CELIS
BEER

BORN IN *Belgium*, BREWED IN *Texas*

JEREMY BANAS

*Forewords by Christine Celis
and Chris Bauweraerts*

Published by American Palate
A Division of The History Press
Charleston, SC
www.historypress.com

Copyright © 2021 by Jeremy Banas
All rights reserved

Front cover: courtesy of Celis Brewery.
Back cover: courtesy of Christine Celis; *logo*: courtesy of Celis Brewery.

First published 2021

ISBN 9781467144360

Library of Congress Control Number: 2020945744

Notice: The information in this book is true and complete to the best of our knowledge. It is offered without guarantee on the part of the author or The History Press. The author and The History Press disclaim all liability in connection with the use of this book.

All rights reserved. No part of this book may be reproduced or transmitted in any form whatsoever without prior written permission from the publisher except in the case of brief quotations embodied in critical articles and reviews.

To my parents, who instilled in me a love of reading, without which I would likely not have gone down the path of writing. Thank you for helping me find one of my passions.

To my boys, Quinn, Jack and Max. Despite all the challenges, no version of the universe exists where I would not want you in my life. You've influenced who I am now and taught me so much more than I think I have ever taught you.

To my darling love, Heidi, to say that you complement me is an understatement; I am whole because of you. Thank you for believing in me, providing guidance and giving me unconditional support during the writing of this book and in life.

CONTENTS

Foreword, by Christine Celis — 7
Foreword, by Chris Bauweraerts — 11
Acknowledgements — 13

Introduction — 15
Part I. Before the Fire: 1966–86 — 21
Part II. After the Fire: 1986–92 — 57
Part III. Texas Bound: 1992–2001 — 67
Part IV. The In-Between Years: 2001–17 — 91
Part V. Modern Times: 2017–present — 101

Appendix I. Belgian Witbier: A Historical Perspective
    with a Focus on Hoegaarden Beer, by Yvan De Baets — 127
Appendix II. A Brief History of Brewing in Hoegaarden — 139
Appendix III. A Brief History of Brewing in Austin, Texas — 147
Appendix IV. Tribute to Pierre, by Rob Tod — 155
Appendix V. Common Beer Terms — 159
Bibliography — 163
Index — 167
About the Author — 173

FOREWORD

What started as a simple idea of my father's in 1965 quickly gained popularity in Europe and in the United States. Today, variations of Pierre Celis's original witbier can be found the world over.

While I am thrilled to see Pierre's vision realized around the globe, I am proud to announce that the Belgian witbier is finally back in its true form. On June 11, 2017, after a seventeen-year hiatus, Celis Brewery once again opened its doors with the launch of Pierre Celis's legacy, the Celis White. When we first opened in 1992, we were the first craft brewery in Austin. Since then, the craft industry has experienced exponential growth, and today, we count ourselves lucky to brew our beers within the vibrant craft community. Within this diverse community, marked by a strong sense of camaraderie, we continue to provide our customers with the quality beers they deserve.

Although most of our fans know this is the second time we have opened Celis Brewery, Austin has grown, and because of that, many people don't know the full story. This book came out of our desire to share the Celis story with you, covering its ups and downs over the years. While keeping in mind our past experiences, we at Celis Brewery are focusing on the future with the release of third-generation, innovative beer styles. Although we take great pride in these new beers, rest assured—our Celis White, Grand Cru, Pale Bock and Raspberry will always remain on tap!

Most important, we look to the future because we understand the meaning behind a beer. A cold Celis White on a hot Texas day is a time-honored way

Foreword, by Christine Celis

Above: Christine and Daytona soon after Celis reopened in 2017, enjoying a Pale Bock. *Courtesy of Celis Brewery.*

Left: From left to right, Christine Celis, Gill Camps and Daytona Camps. *Courtesy of the author.*

Foreword, by Christine Celis

to connect with friends and family. I started this brewery to pass on the family legacy to my children, Gill and Daytona, and they know as well as I do that a brewery is about much more than making great beer. This is a "people" business—and we all love being with people. So please come visit us. It would be our pleasure to give you a tour and show you our beer garden!

We hope you enjoy reading this book as much as we have enjoyed brewing pint after pint.

Proost!

—Christine Celis

FOREWORD

Pierre Celis changed my life in the spring of '77, when I had the pleasure to taste for the first time a turbid beer previously unknown to me: the Oud Hoegaerds. That moment is still the greatest "wow" moment for my tastebuds in all my life.

A few days later, I drove with my car to the Vroentestraat in Hoegaarden. There was the very tiny Brouwerij Celis. There I stowed my car with sixteen cases of Oud-Hoegaerds. Pierre Celis was very surprised to see a consumer driving to his brewery to buy sixteen cases of his Oud Hoegaerds. Since then, we meet regularly, at the beginning, in Hoegaarden, later, in Achouffe. When Pierre tasted for the first time La Chouffe, he advised us to add coriander to La Chouffe. Very good advice.

We had some things in common.

Both breweries, the Celis Brewery and Brasserie d'Achouffe, started to brew in old copper washtubs of one-hundred-liter capacity that were recycled as tiny brew kettles.

In 1991, the Belgian brew equipment company Les Ateliers de Monsville started to build the Achouffe Brewhouse. We were invited to visit our future brewhouse at this Belgian manufactory, and we were very surprised to see the future brew equipment of the Celis Brewery in Austin. The two brewhouses started operation in 1992, one in Achouffe and the other in Austin.

The American Celis Brewery quickly gained a reputation in the U.S. world of beer. One year after the start of the production of Celis White, Pierre experienced his best memory in the beer world. Pierre was invited

Foreword, by Chris Bauweraerts

to speak at the congress of the National American Brewers Association in Seattle, Washington. Practically all of the American brewers attended this conference. Pierre told me that he was "trembling in his legs."

History should remember that Pierre Celis was the first Belgian brewer to start a Belgian-inspired brewery in the United States. I remember that Pierre was a very gentle and humble person. He was always ready to help and advised other breweries. As a brewer and an entrepreneur, Pierre Celis is my godfather. I was very lucky that our paths crossed.

Here are some of my favorite quotes from Pierre Celis:

"All my life I did business in white products, first as a local milk distributor, then as brewer of 'white' Beer."

"I like Texas as the people there speak slowly, so I can understand them easier."

"When it smells well in the fermentation room, then I know that I am in a good brewery."

"Why should I pay for malted wheat if I can use unmalted wheat?"

"Cows don't eat grapes, that's why cheese pairs better with beer."

"All good things come from Belgium: waffles, chocolates, beer, fries and eclairs."

I will always remember him.

—Chris Bauweraerts,
April 27, 2020

ACKNOWLEDGEMENTS

*T*his is always the most difficult part of a book for me. There are so many people who helped and supported the writing of this book. How can I possibly mention them all without forgetting a person or two? Regardless, here it goes.

Christine Celis, Daytona and Gill Camps. That you let me into your family's life, and history, is truly humbling. I cannot fully express how much I appreciate you entrusting me with telling the story. I have found good friends and kindred spirits with the three of you. Thank you for everything.

Juliette Celis. It was truly the highlight of my trip, getting to spend the afternoon with you and listening to your stories of Pierre, as well as your involvement with the brewery. You are one fantastic lady.

Chris Bauweraerts. You have become a friend and inspiration. I enjoyed (and still do) our talks of all things Belgian, beer and life. Your help with this book has been incredible. Thank you for your wisdom, knowledge and friendship.

Luc Vanderplas. Thank you for the time you took while I was in Belgium researching this book, to talk with me about your time working with Pierre and your friendship with him. I have enjoyed staying in touch with you and call you my friend as well.

Miel Mattheus. You were one of the few who stood by Pierre when he left De Kluis. Your dedication to him and what he stood for is a true testament to your character. Thank you for sharing your stories.

Acknowledgements

Frank Boon. You have certainly in your own right earned a place in Belgian beer history. Thank you for taking the time to talk with me at your brewery about your interactions with Pierre. I truly enjoyed our talk, as well as your delicious lambics and guezes!

Sean Elfstrom. That was quite a time we had on the "Banas Belgian Beer Tour." Thank you for coming with me on an epic tour of the Netherlands and Belgium while I conducted the initial research for this book. Most of all, thank you for taking the driving duties during the trip. One of these days, I'll learn to drive a manual transmission.

Bert Van Heck. I think I have found my brewing soul mate with you. I could spend hours talking beer history with you. You truly are one of the most talented and innovative brewers around.

Rob Tod. I've thrown around the notion of "kindred spirit" already in these acknowledgments. I've truly enjoyed our talks about Celis, beer and whatever comes to mind. Thank you for not beating me over the head for bugging you at any given moment, even during Zoom panels with Vinnie and Jan.

Martha and Greta Arnauts. Thank you for taking the time to talk with me and for helping me speak with Juliette. It was a pleasure to speak with both of you.

Travis Poling. Thank you for continuing to be a mentor, as well as a good friend.

Arianna Auber. Thank you for going over what I had written and making sure that it all made sense, as well as your assistance with parts of Austin's beer history. Your help is much appreciated.

Mike Smith. Thank you for making me aware of a photo that I feel was integral to this book.

Yvan de Baets. I've met a fellow beer historian in you. Your dedication to researching and preserving beer history is nothing short of incredible.

Ben Gibson, Rick Delaney and everyone at The History Press/Arcadia Publishing. Your support and guidance has been a blessing.

Paul Vega and Marco Ortega. Thank you both for being sounding boards for ideas on this book, and for just being you.

To those who took valuable time from their schedules to sit for interviews with me: Billy Forrester, Wayne Kleck, Dally Vuletich, Jason Davis (you're welcome), Kim Clarke, Peter Camps, Pete Slosberg, Garret Oliver, Chris Black, Bert Van Hecke, Brock Wagner, Bobo Van Mechelen, Bob Legget, Jim Houchins, James Hudec and so many more.

INTRODUCTION

To understand Pierre Celis and his importance, one must understand Hoegaarden and Belgium's love affair with beer. Though beer is the national beverage of Belgium, even by Belgian standards Hoegaarden is special when it comes to our favorite malted beverage.

Hoegaarden sits tucked away in Belgium's Flemish Brabant area of the Flanders region, and its present population, including two nearby municipalities, stands at around eight thousand people. This cozy little town celebrated its one thousandth year in 2018, though it can trace its origins to around AD 600, when the noblewoman Ermelindis was given a sign by God that she would need to settle in the nearby town of Meldert, thus beginning the establishment of settlements in the area, including Hoegaarden.

Settlement of Hoegaarden dates to around the second century, when trade routes connected the modern town of Tienen—then known as Gallo-Romas Vicus—with the town of Nivelles.

A more formal founding of Hoegaarden, and the surrounding area, came less than one thousand years later. The Hoegaarden area quickly established itself as an agricultural community; farmland and canals were constructed. Nearby water sources made this easy, giving future brewers a water source for their beer. Although breweries in Hoegaarden likely came into existence prior to the twelfth century, it was by 1318 that breweries would likely have already been in place. The first documented brewery, in 1460, was founded by the Beggaarden brothers in the Mariadal area of Hoegaarden.

Introduction

Between 1460 and 1794, brewing in Hoegaarden thrived, partially due to tax breaks residents received from the government, allowing exponential growth within the industry. During this period, Hoegaarden boasted dozens of breweries that produced a number of styles, but mainly what would become the area's famous witbier.

The number of breweries in Hoegaarden began to decline after 1794, likely due to the lack of friendly tax laws for brewers. This by no means meant that beer was not still a mainstay of the town and its area residents. Quite the contrary; beer was still life itself. Locals even talk about French troops coming through Belgium in the eighteenth century attempting to march through Hoegaarden on their way to Germany. Town leaders met the French troops and bribed them with, you guessed it, beer. Well, it worked. The French troops marched around Hoegaarden.

Fast-forwarding to the early twentieth century, Hoegaarden was down to only nine breweries by 1914, a number that would be reduced to four after the end of the First World War. Of these four, one in particular stood out: Brouwerij Tomsin. The Tomsin Brewery, like most in the area, was a farmhouse brewery, one that happened to be next door to the childhood home of Pierre Celis. Its proximity would have long-lasting effects on the young milkman.

It is rare to come across an individual who defines an entire category or genre on their own. To be known for one thing that spreads like wildfire around the globe, influencing us to the point that we think only of them when we speak of it, is generation-spanning defining.

Bear in mind that at this time, though witbier was gone from Hoegaarden, it was not extinct as an overall style. The Hoegaards beer (as it was known) was one of three different types of witbiers (Flemish for white beers) in Belgium. In addition to the Hoegaarden variety, there was the Lueven Wit and the Peeterman Wit, both popular as well throughout Belgium. It would be the Hoegaards version that was the more popular of the three, with Hoegaarden distributing a ton of its beer to Lueven itself at one point. It was Hoegaarden that was most spoken of in Belgium.

For almost two decades after Pierre opened his brewery in Hoegaarden, while the Lueven and Peeterman Wits were still in limited production elsewhere, Pierre's business was growing. By the end of the 1970s, the Lueven Wit would die out, with the Peeterman variety following in the 1980s.

This only serves to add to the legend of Pierre Celis, the "Godfather of the Witbier." For though his Oud Hoegaards was not the only style of witbier historically when he opened his brewery in 1966, it became the only

Introduction

one any of us knows today. Pierre singlehandedly outlasted those brewing the Lueven and Peeterman versions, and his Oud Hoegaards style became what the entire world today defines as a witbier. The Leuven and Peeterman varieties became nothing more than a faded memory. For more on this, refer to Appendix I.

Pierre Celis did not invent the witbier style. No, the cloudy wheat beer native to southern Belgium that graces almost every brewery and pub in the world has been around for more than four hundred years. Garrett Oliver, brewmaster for Brooklyn Brewing, put it this way: "We can't point to somebody and say they were the progenitor of the triple or even the IPA, or whatever else. But in Pierre's case, he may not have invented witbier, but he pretty much invented it for everybody who brews it now." This is Pierre's legacy.

Pierre was a businessman and an innovator. He loved to tinker with things and share his passion with others. Nothing was ever impossible for Pierre. He considered what others thought to be impossible as a challenge, as something that was impossible only for now, until he was able to conquer it.

In many ways, the story is well known. A milkman in the southern Belgian town of Hoegaarden leaves his family's dairy business to open a brewery and, in the process, resurrects a style that had died out only a decade before. Pierre was still a milkman when he began to tinker with brewing again. At the time, he was still devoted to the family dairy business and had not thought of brewing again. But the townspeople of Hoegaarden, Belgium, had other ideas.

Hoegaarden has been around for one thousand years, with beer a part of the town's fabric for almost half that time. In Hoegaarden, to not be brewing the witbier they were known for, let alone not brewing at all, was unheard of.

When the Brouwerij Tomsin closed in 1957, Hoegaarden and the surrounding areas were devastated. Three to four years would go by before the citizens of this perfect little town in southern Belgium began to wonder how they could have their coveted witbier and bring brewing back to Hoegaarden. Fortunately for them, they knew just the person to bring them back to brewing prominence.

Pierre Celis had worked as an apprentice brewer at the Tomsin Brewery in the 1950s while a teenager. He learned everything there was to know about witbier and brewing in general from Louis Tomsin, who took Pierre under his wing, setting himself up perfectly for when thirsty citizens of Hoegaarden came calling, asking Pierre to brew the witbier he'd learned to master at Tomsin Brewery.

Introduction

The infamous Louis Tomsin, Pierre's first teacher and mentor, in 1957, the year his brewery closed. *Courtesy of Christine Celis.*

Pierre did many test batches in secret at the family farm and home and, by 1965, was ready to open the first brewery in Hoegaarden in eight years. By 1966, Pierre had opened the first Celis Brewery at his home, much the way it had been done for centuries in his hometown and throughout Belgium. If you saw a smokestack, chances are a brewery was there.

It did not take long for word of Pierre's achievement to reach folks in his hometown and throughout Belgium. What had started as a historic regional beer was soon to become a global phenomenon, though Pierre had no intention of this.

Pierre was a humble man who did not seek fortune and glory. No, Pierre saw himself more as a public servant. He was doing something that he loved, and all he cared about was that people shared his passion and enjoyed the beer he produced. It was important to Pierre that he had not only brought back the first new brewery in Hoegaarden in nine years but also that he was bringing back the witbier style Hoegaarden was known for.

Over the next twenty years, Pierre's brewery grew exponentially, selling beers throughout Europe and grabbing the attention of people in the United States. By the mid-1980s, most folks in Europe knew what a witbier was, and many breweries had one of their own on tap. What had been for centuries

Introduction

just a regional beer in Flemish Brabant had not only been brought back from extinction but had also been brought to international prominence.

It wasn't enough for Pierre just to manage his brewery and focus on his product. He also wanted to help others who needed it. Chris Bauweraerts, founder of Aschouffe Brewing in southern Belgium, credits Pierre for not only helping him get started but also supporting him as he grew and for being a continuing mentor willing to share his knowledge of beer and what it takes to run a brewery.

This was Pierre—a salesman for sure, passionate about his craft, but also a man of the people. Pierre wanted to spread his passion as far and wide as he possibly could. When he was forced to divest his shares in his own brewery to a company then known as InBev, Pierre looked to the only other place that made sense: the United States.

Pierre's love for everything American was well known, and he saw the United States as the future for his brewing endeavors, even before he sold his brewery in Hoegaarden to InBev. Pierre found the people of Texas and Austin very welcoming for what he was trying to do. It didn't hurt that his Belgian witbier was the perfect refreshing beer for the Texas climate.

The world was now enamored with witbier, and it wanted more. More witbier, more Pierre, and the scrappy little Belgian was more than happy to oblige the world. He felt a sense of responsibility to show others what he had done and how so that they too could fulfill their dreams. Pierre was a lover of people and was determined to make sure they lived their best lives.

It has been a true honor to write the story.

—Jeremy Banas

Part I
BEFORE THE FIRE

1966–86

EARLY LIFE AND BREWING BEGINNINGS

Hoegaarden, Belgium, is a community built on beer. This sleepy little village is just over one thousand years old now, and beer has been part of its history dating all the way back to the early fourteenth century. Hoegaarden is in the diocese of Liège, smack dab in the middle of the Flemish Brabant area of Belgium. It's known for its agriculture as well as its beer.

Pierre Celis was born on March 21, 1925, in Hoegaarden to Ernest Celis and his wife, Victorine Peeters. The family home at that time was just a small corner house near the village's municipal square. As with most town squares, Hoegaarden's was the center of activity. The town hall, taverns and the village's beautiful gothic church are all easily viewed from the square. All these hearken back to a time when life was less hectic, though most Belgians work hard to keep a relaxed lifestyle.

Around the time Pierre was one year old, his father purchased what would become the family home for the rest of his life, a modest farmhouse on Vroentestraat not far from the Nermbeek and next to the Tomsin home and brewery. This would prove to be a most fortuitous move on his father's part. By this point, the Celis family had been in Hoegaarden for a few generations. Pierre's grandfather came to Hoegaarden from another small town about five miles from Hoegaarden, the village of Hauthem. They were true Hoegaardiers (as local residents are known), to be sure. Their recent family history saw the Celis clan as cattle merchants by trade, a mantle

Celis Beer

Map of Belgium, with inset of the Hoegaarden in the Flemish Brabant region. *Illustration by Meagan Garrett based on maps from Google and Rough Guides.*

Pierre himself, as well as his two brothers, Walter and Virgil, would take up for a time. All three boys would jump into the family business at an early age.

Pierre was a happy child. At an early age, the Celis children were trained in the family business, which included some dairy production. Pierre, Walter and Virgil, as well as their mother, Victorine, often helped milk the cows or whatever was needed, including making butter, though butter was not a moneymaker.

Before the Fire

His schooling was not neglected, however. Pierre went to elementary school in Hoegaarden at a school run by monks. In his teens, he attended a French-speaking school in the town of Jodoigne and would often ride his bike to and from school, regardless of the season. It's common to this day for Belgian children to learn several languages during their primary years, and Pierre was no different. But he tired of rotating languages during his schooling. At the age of seventeen, he left school. "My motivation to get a diploma had vanished," he said. "I'd rather enter the business world," he says in the collection of interviews known as *Pierre Celis: My Life*.

Pierre became involved with the local milk organization AA, supplying his milk to area hospitals, including military hospitals, as well as public service organizations and retail outlets. Though it wasn't his life's passion at the time, in true Pierre style, he threw himself into the quality of his product.

Despite his success at rechartering the family cattle ranch into a dairy farm, Pierre realized it was ultimately not meant to be. Larger dairy companies would make life hard for small-town Belgian dairy farmers. Pierre didn't wish for his family heritage with cattle and dairy to wind down, but the fact that it did would eventually work to his advantage.

Pierre had developed a solid work ethic growing up and didn't mind the cattle business. But it wasn't his passion.

With Louis Tomsin next door, a teenage Pierre often found himself at his neighbor's brewery. He soon found that this profession interested him far more than did the cattle trade. Around 1945, a young Pierre spent time with Tomsin at his brewery, and Pierre was put to work stirring barrels of wort. Observation over the years allowed Pierre to pick up other parts of the brewing process, and he was hooked. It seems to have run in the family: Pierre's grandfather on his mother's side, Jean Liévin Peeters, was a brewery worker at DuPont Brewing on Stoopkenstraat in Hoegaarden a number of years before Pierre was born.

Louis Tomsin was an interesting man, even by Belgian standards. Life was hard for Tomsin, and he was often intoxicated, a condition that Pierre says he blamed the whole neighborhood for. He did not eat or sleep well. Despite this tough exterior and approach to life, one thing was certain: He loved young Pierre, often referring to him as the giant of Flanders, a reference to Pierre's short stature.

Tomsin did not have any children and looked to Pierre to carry the torch. Though he did not do so right away, the gesture was still not lost on Pierre, and he almost considered brewing when Tomsin closed. "He always called

A young Pierre and Juliette.
Courtesy of Christine Celis.

me 'géant de Flanders, the giant of Flanders' because I was a short skinny guy," says Pierre in *Pierre Celis: My Life*.

When World War II came around, Pierre's older brother, Virgil Celis, served in the Belgian army. Pierre, no longer a teenager, stayed and helped his father at the farm, though at some point during these years, he escaped to France to work on a farm with family, says Pierre's daughter, Christine. Pierre's younger brother, Walter, would not join him in France, as he was eight years younger and not old enough to go. Pierre returned to Hoegaarden after the war and rejoined the family business. It was not long after Pierre returned that the last witbier brewery in Hoegaarden closed.

In 1953, Pierre married a young Juliette Vanlangendonck. Juliette grew up in the village of Meldert, the daughter of a blacksmith. Pierre had met Juliette at a dance in Meldert and was instantly smitten. Pierre courted young Juliette for a number of years. Juliette moved into Pierre's family home on Vroentestraat after the wedding.

When Brouwerij Tomsin closed in 1957, Pierre was devastated. Tomsin was not just a neighbor to the Celis family, but Pierre's brewing mentor as

Before the Fire

Taken in the 1930s, this photo shows Louis Tomsin (*top left*) and his brewing crew: Henri Finoulst (*top, second from left, and father to Martha Arnauts*), Pierre Celis (*top, second from right*), Jef Homblé (*top right*) and Emile Koekelkoren (*bottom left*). Note the position Pierre is in, as well as how he is holding the basket. Keep this in mind when looking at the below photograph. *Courtesy of Café Brem.*

One of the brewers stands with a brewing basket over Luis Tomsin's mash tun at the Open Air Museum in Bokrijk, Belgium. (The brewer is in the same position as the young Pierre in the previous picture). The mash tun was moved to Bokrijk soon after Tomsin's brewery closed in 1957. This equipment was what Pierre Celis apprenticed on in his teens. *Courtesy of the author.*

Tomsin's mash tun and lauter tank in Bokrijk. *Courtesy of the author.*

well. Though the Loriers Brewery was still open at the time, the last of the witbier brewers were gone. Loriers brewed lager beer. For a town that was known for beer and as the best source of witbier specifically, this was devastating. Tomsin's brewing equipment was later sold to the open-air museum in Bokrijklaan (Bokrij), Belgium, where it remains today.

The equipment of Louis Tomsin, which now rests in the museum of Bokrij, was first thought to be from a brewery in Diependaal, in the province of Limburg, not far from Bokrijk. During a museum visit in the early 1970s, Pierre discovered that Tomsin's equipment was not getting the credit it deserved at Bokrijk. Along with friends, such as Luc Vanderplas from Hoegaarden, he protested loudly that the wrong brewery was listed.

Pierre would go so far as to hold a press conference, complete with photos, supporting the claim that the equipment was in fact Tomsin's. Eventually, Tomsin was recognized, and the museum made the name change.

Time was moving on as it always had, and it was taking Hoegaarden with it. Many feared the beverage that had given the town its identity would never return. The townspeople of Hoegaarden would not soon forget, though. In many ways, they refused to move on. Other witbier styles from neighboring towns such as Leuven and Tienen were available in Hoegaarden for sure, but to this sleepy little town, it was a matter of pride. It didn't matter that the residents could still obtain beer. Not brewing their Oud Hoegaards beer remained a sore spot.

Pierre Gets Down to Business

Around 1960, talk in Hoegaarden began to center on bringing beer back. The problem was that no one seemed willing to take the leap to open a brewery, including people in neighboring towns. There were many reasons why breweries had closed down in recent years, and many people remembered that Pierre had worked at the Tomsin Brewery little more than a decade before, in his teens. Pierre began to be gently nudged by those in town to brew their witbier. After all, he not only knew how to brew, he also knew how to brew the Oud (old in Flemish) Hoegaards beer, their witbier.

Many in the village did not think Pierre could accomplish this goal, fearing that Tomsin's recipe was buried with the old brewer. Pierre knew otherwise, for he had observed Tomsin closely. He watched Tomsin obtain his water from the brook running through the streets and saw where he obtained his grain. Pierre watched every step of the process.

After more than a little push, Pierre began to take the suggestion to heart. In fact, he saw an opportunity. Starting out in one of the cowsheds at the family farm on Vroentestraat in Hoegaarden, Pierre took a dairy kettle and began to quietly experiment at his home. He did it so quietly, in fact, that his beloved bride, Juliette, had no idea what he was attempting. Of course, Pierre had to see if he could make this work. He had no doubt he could reproduce the witbier Louis Tomsin had taught him; it was just a matter of time, after all, and determining the best course of action to launch a brewery was the next step.

To get started, Pierre obtained an old wine barrel from a nearby distillery and cut it in half, creating a false bottom with holes for filtration of the grain. He then contacted Tomsin's old carpenter, Albert Mannaerts, who adjusted the equipment to allow Pierre to brew up to two hundred liters of beer.

Those first few batches of witbier, prior to getting yeast, did not go quite as Pierre expected. He followed Tomsin's recipe exactly, but after several days, there were no signs of active fermentation. Something was wrong, and Pierre knew it. What happened, he wondered? In addition to the recipe, Pierre knew he'd followed the techniques taught to him.

To help solve this little mystery, Pierre turned to another retired brewer for help: Marcel Thomas of the former Loriers Brewery. After listening to Pierre describe the process he had gone through when brewing, Thomas asked him if he had remembered to add the yeast. Alas, Pierre advised, he had not. Pierre had never seen Louis Tomsin add yeast to his beers; as such, it never occurred to him. After the beer had been brewed and cooled, Tomsin would transfer it straight into barrels for fermentation.

Since it had never been explained to him, Pierre did not account for residual wild yeast that had made its home in the barrels. Though Pierre was an astute observer of the process, this part he missed. This is where Tomsin obtained the yeast to ferment his beer, Thomas explained. This made sense to Pierre. Though he had learned the recipe and the process, it had been many years since he had brewed it. Thomas was more than happy to supply Pierre with his initial yeast from Loriers, itself obtained by Thomas from the Whitbread Brewery in England. It was a blend of Scottish and English yeasts.

At times, Loriers did not have any extra yeast for Pierre, so Pierre contacted Raymond Moreau at Mont Saint Gilbert Brewery to get his yeast. "Supplementing from time to time, the yeast he would get from Loriers," says Christine Celis, Pierre's daughter. "I remember as a little girl taking milk jugs with my dad to Mont Saint Gilbert and filling them with yeast." This hybrid Scottish/Belgian yeast from Brasserie Mont Saint Guibert was easily modified and would allow for continued consistency of his beers, as well as a very similar flavor profile.

It was on one of these occasions, years later, when Pierre would need help from Mont Saint Gilbert. He stole away in the middle of the night to meet Raymond (who provided the yeast without the knowledge of his bosses), and once the yeast was obtained, he headed home to Hoegaarden, adding in the yeast. Once again, Pierre, the "Flemish Fox," won out, and Raymond was able to hide his deed from his superiors.

After this initial obstacle with the yeast, Pierre began to nail down his recipe and disburse bottles of his beer to town residents, telling them that it was the last of the Tomsin witbier so as to not unduly influence them. It worked. All were ecstatic with the beer, and no one realized that it was Pierre's. Marcel Thomas knew the truth, and he told Pierre his beer would be a bestseller for sure. Pierre eventually let slip it was his, and Hoegaarden was ecstatic, quickly embracing the new beer.

Before the Fire

A young Christine with Pierre in 1967.
Courtesy of Christine Celis.

For a while, Pierre quietly brewed his witbier just for Hoegaarden. So quietly, in fact, that everyone in the town knew except his wife, Juliette. "People from the village would come to our dairy farm with milk jugs, and Pierre would happily fill them," said Juliette. "Little did I know that he was filling these jugs with his beer. Everyone in the town knew, it seemed, except for me!"

Pierre may have had good reason to keep this a secret from his wife, for though she supported her husband in all he did, she was not a fan of him getting back into the beer world. Perhaps this was due to the unpredictable nature of the business at that point in Hoegaarden. A dairy farm or a cattle business surely would be more stable.

Even Pierre's longtime childhood friend (and now neighbor) Martha knew what Pierre was doing. Since it was known that Juliette did not want her husband to get back into brewing, this secret was very closely kept. No one in the village wanted the beer to disappear again! Eventually, Juliette found out what her husband was doing and quickly realized this was his passion. She also realized that this harebrained idea of his just might work.

Even in 1960s Belgium, there was paperwork to complete in order to open a new business. In 1946, Pierre rechartered the family cattle business to a dairy farm. In 1965, as he was formulating his plans to open the brewery, he applied with the local town council to again recharter the business, this time into a brewery. On June 1, 1966, he received his brewer's license issued by the county council. The license allowed for one boil kettle, one mash tun, two oil burners and five electric motors with nine horsepower each.

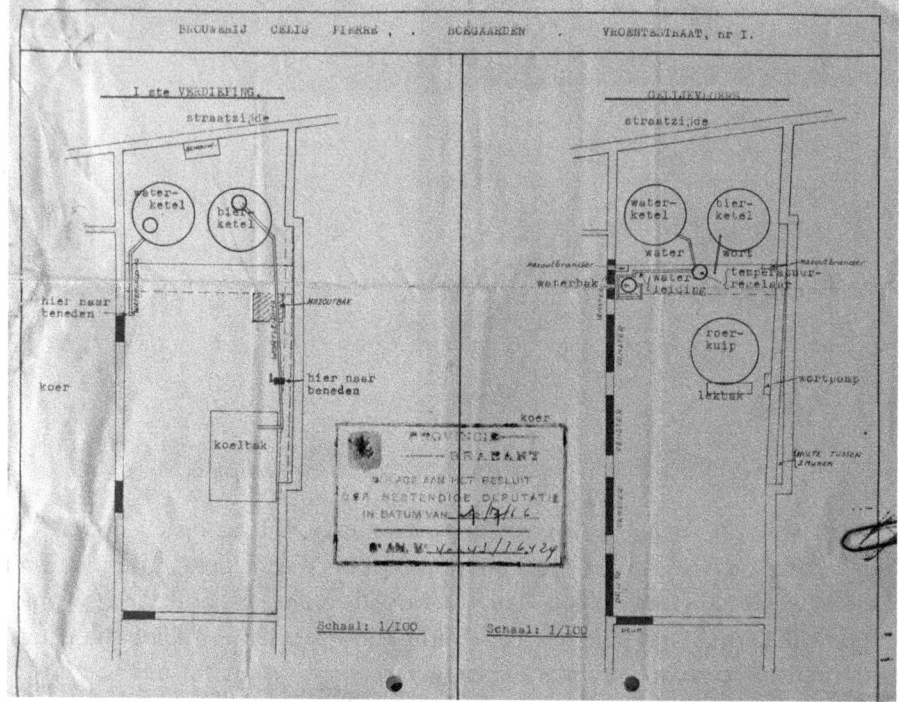

Pierre's original plans for the farmhouse brewery (Brouwerij Celis), July 7, 1966. *Courtesy of the author.*

At this point, he had most of what he needed to open the brewery. Taking his knowledge of sanitation and horizontal tanks from his now-former dairy business, along with a little borrowed capital, Pierre purchased brewing equipment from the Zolder Brewery for around $1,500 in Flemish francs and opened his brewery doors for business in 1966.

Little did Pierre know at the time that the equipment he had purchased from Zolder had quite a storied history. Manufactured by Usine Meura in Tournai, Belgium, in 1914, Pierre's equipment had initially been purchased by a female brewer in Belgium, which was behind enemy lines at the time. Not long after the brewer took possession of her equipment, German soldiers came to her farm brewery and stayed for a while, taking advantage of her food, beer and hospitality. During World War I, German soldiers took the copper brewing equipment and brought it back to Germany, as copper was highly prized by the Germans during the war.

Not content to stand for this, she snuck over into Germany and stole her equipment back, making it the only copper brewing system in Belgium

Before the Fire

A copy of the contract between Pierre and government officials in Hoegaarden, rechartering his family's dairy farm to that of a brewery. *Courtesy of the author.*

to survive World War I. It's quite a story, and it seems like fate that the equipment would later land in the hands of a man who would forever change brewing worldwide.

Armed with the new equipment, Pierre still had to tackle a few obstacles. Knowledgeable though he was, he had gaps in this knowledge. He was smart enough to know what he did not know, and he sought out those who could help. Pierre used his natural talent for relating to people to get this assistance. Though he sought out expertise when needed, Pierre had the brewing process down just fine (outside of that little yeast hiccup). He was supremely confident that he would succeed. "I was not a brewing engineer," he says in *My Life*, "but I surrounded myself with people such as Mister Thomas. These people were more learned than I was, and they had highly professional skills."

Despite Pierre's optimism, tax officials and others were not as optimistic as the little milkman was. Many gave Pierre six months before he was out of business. Some, like the brewers at the Alken Brewery, had no faith in him at all. After all, many other breweries had recently closed their doors,

Christine Celis stands next to her father's original mash tun, which was altered by Pierre after purchase. The mash tun will be part of the Celis Brewery's brewing museum dedicated to Celis' history and traditional Belgian brewing techniques. *Courtesy of Celis Brewing.*

like Marcel Thomas's Lories Brewery in Hoegaarden, the Grisar Brewery in Linter and several in the villages of Kerkom and Eliksem.

The larger industrial breweries, such as Stella Artois, were acquiring smaller breweries and then closing them, often to avoid competition. Though these acquisitions left only breweries of lager beer, they also left a gap for Pierre Celis. It seems these giants of the brewing world felt they could better dictate to the palates of Belgian and European drinkers. Many formerly independent brands became massive as a result.

As Pierre and his crew assembled their brewery, Pierre started out with the traditional wooden barrels for delivery of the finished beer. However, he soon traded up to stainless steel barrels, acquiring ten in the beginning from the Comet barrel factory in Mechelen. Pierre recollects that the manager of the factory laughed a little at this, as it had been some time since anyone had started a brewery from the ground up. This was intriguing to many.

That first year saw Pierre and the Celis Brewery produce a little less than 350 barrels of witbier (approximately 300 hectoliters). Despite this efficiency, much of the equipment and process were manual. Pierre did not have the luxury of automation. In the absence of a motorized pump, Pierre and his helpers hand cranked the pumps. Those who distributed his beer often stayed to help with part of the brewing process, though Pierre would sometimes sneak out for a slice of bread in his kitchen while they finished up.

PIERRE RAMPS UP BREWING

Having established that there was interest in his beer among his fellow Hoegaardiers, Pierre began to sell his wares to private individuals. Many would still come by with empty milk jugs to be filled with beer to take home, much like today's growlers; other neighbors would buy barrels and tap them at home. His beer was selling like hotcakes, as Thomas predicted it would.

Soon after, interest in nearby Tienen sprouted up, with private individuals asking for the beer, and the interest certainly did not stop there. Pierre's father, Ernest, was in the village of Jodoigne patronizing a local bar (or cafés, as they are known in Belgium) and left having persuaded the owners to become Pierre's first retail client.

Not everyone ordered ahead of time. One day early on at the brewery, Pierre opened his door to a surprise. A Belgian from the Zuyderzee region

Pierre in front of his original equipment at Brouwerij Celis, the farmhouse brewery, in 1968. *Courtesy of Christine Celis.*

had just stopped by, out of the blue, wanting beer. Not having expected this order, Pierre was caught off guard and did not have any extra beer for sale. But there's little doubt that Pierre did not turn him away. He probably still took the man's order and delivered the beer at a later date.

Pierre's witbier even showed up in the popular tourist town of Antwerp, some seventy-five kilometers north of Hoegaarden, at the local café Vagant in the Haarlem area of town. At first, Pierre delivered crates of beer (as he already had bottles) to Vagant. After his first delivery, he was called out the next day to deliver more beer—this time, multiple barrels. Going forward, Vagant's proprietor would come to Hoegaarden to pick up beer from Pierre on a regular basis.

Pierre hired local schoolteacher Albert Guilluy to drill a well at the Vroente. The well was drilled at a depth of eighteen meters, and at this depth, the water almost gushed into the air. When Pierre later moved his brewery to nearby Stoopkensstraat Street, he was able to use the already drilled well water there.

Pierre also needed help running day-to-day operations. To solve this problem, he often used relatives and friends, most of whom were more than happy to help with work that was done by hand. One friend, Jules Ons in Leuven, imported bottle fillers. Using primarily second-use bottles, the machine required someone to manually lace each bottle under the filler, which would fill it up with beer, then manually place lead caps on them by pressing a lever with their foot. This was accomplished by Pierre himself or friends.

When, later, Pierre added a separate bottling building—purchased for the modest sum of $5,000 (Belgian francs) in Limburg—it was Pierre's mother who washed the bottles and stuck the labels on them by hand. Pierre's wife, Juliette, cleaned the stainless-steel barrels, and she also helped with the bottles. Even Juliette's uncle Victor, who had previously worked at a brewery, lent a hand.

To help with distribution, Pierre had friends, like local historians Josef Wijns and Jan Lambin, bring bottles to their friends and colleagues. Around this time, a friend who would become pivotal for Pierre going forward, Luc Vanderplas, came into the picture. Luc wore many hats over the years in his time with Pierre, not only helping with distribution of bottles and barrels but also serving as essentially a one-man marketing machine. The term *brand ambassador* does not do justice to the efforts Luc put in.

Luc wasn't an official employee of Pierre's, despite the years he worked with him at both Brouwerij Celis and Brouwerij De Kluis. Luc was a huge fan of what Pierre was doing, as well as being a fellow Hoegaardier. At one point, Luc played in a band with fellow Belgians, who wrote songs about Pierre and his beer. Even after Pierre left Hoegaarden to open a brewery in Texas, Luc continued to fight for him.

By the mid-1960s, Hoegaarden was a village of around six thousand residents and had enjoyed a storied history with beer. Pierre was hoping to keep this tradition. (He hoped, however, not to have to bribe invading armies with beer to march around Hoegaarden, as his ancestors had done in the 1700s with French troops.)

In 1967, Pierre released one of his more popular beers, one that is still highly regarded in Belgium, as well as at the new Celis Brewery in Austin. (Hold tight, we will get to that one later.) Pierre was looking for an expression that would fall in line with the monasteries of Belgium. Enter Celis Grand Cru, his take on a tripel, or trippel, a much stronger and maltier beer. These specialty beers allowed Pierre to realize a larger profit, leading to the ability to borrow more money, obtain new partners and, thus, expand.

By 1968, just two years removed from the brewery's opening, advertising for the Celis Brewery was ramping up. Local bars like Café 't Nieuwhuys, and Café Brem, both of which date back centuries, proudly advertised Pierre and the return of their beloved witbier. In advertising its own establishment, Café 't Nieuwhuys proudly mentioned that it served the white beer from the Celis Brewery: "a unique tavern to enjoy the Blonde Hoegaarden Beer of Brewery Celis."

Another advertising stratagem, employed by Pierre, was the tried-and-true practice of giveaways. When festivals or parties were being planned, he often gave a barrel of his beer to the festivities. Though that practice may have taken away from what he could sell, it was in many ways a lot cheaper than employing two or three sales reps to promote the beer. The goodwill this produced was invaluable.

All of this success had a price. It required more and more of Pierre and of those helping him. It was not enough to brew the beer. By handling his own distribution, Pierre was always on the move. Of course, he loved this. He relished being out in the field, so to speak, interacting with his customers and bar owners. However, as demand ramped up, he needed help with distribution. Fortunately for Pierre, some café owners would come to his farmhouse brewery to pick up crates of bottles to take back and sell at their establishments.

One such individual was a young Frank Boon, a native of Merchtem, located fifteen kilometers northwest of Brussels. Boon was looking to expand

Before the Fire

Advertisements for Hoegaarden Grand Cru decorate the gates of a restaurant in Hoegaarden, early 1980s. *Courtesy of Christine Celis.*

A Celis Grand Cru delivery truck in the early 1980s. *Courtesy of Christine Celis.*

Left: A Hoegaarden Wit brewed at today's Brouwerij De Kluis, at Café Brem, just two doors down from the brewery. *Courtesy of the author.*

Below: Patrons at Café Brem, in Hoegaarden, enjoying their witbier early in the morning. Café Brem is located next to Brouwerij De Kluis. God bless Belgium. *Courtesy of the author.*

Before the Fire

Pierre and Juliette's home on Stoopkensstraat (Stoopken Street) in Hoegaarden, Belgium, the original site of Brouwerij Celis, prior to its move to the Hougardia lemonade factory in 1979. *Courtesy of the author.*

his fledgling distribution business by selling specialty beers. To get more familiar with the breweries of the mid-1970s, Boon grabbed a brewing guide that included all the existing breweries, suppliers, distributors and the like. He set out to tour Belgium, intent on seeing what knowledge he could gain from those still around. It was during this trip that, in 1975, Boon met Pierre, who had been brewing for almost a decade.

After trying Pierre's witbier, Boon was hooked. But it was not enough for just him to enjoy it. Boon wanted others to as well. He hadn't been in the market for table beers like the wit; he instead had been looking for specialty beers. But he wanted to help distribute beers from Brouwerij Celis. "I had an agreement with Pierre, and I went to Hoegaarden to pick up, say, twelve or fourteen pallets of beer, and he made an agreement with his guy that he would open the gate at 4:30 or 5:00 in the morning, before all the others," says Boon. "So, I came there, opened the gate, and I served myself a truck full of pallets. Then I would come back at 6:30, and by 7:00 or 7:30, we were ready to head to Brussels," Boon advised. "In the beginning, I was driving my truck myself, I had a few guys working at my brewery, but I tried to save as much money as possible."

This system helped to spread the beers of both Pierre's brewery and many small Belgian breweries. Brewers, who today be referred to as craft brewers, at this time in the mid-1970s were referred to as artists, likely jump-starting the term *artisanal* around the world as a marketing term for small, hand-crafted items.

Perhaps part of Pierre's appeal outside of southern Belgium was the lighter color of white beer and its similarity to lager beer in that regard. It's easier to get a lager drinker to convert to something like a Belgian white beer or a Belgian Golden Strong than darker beers or traditional sour beers such as lambics.

Though Boon was also starting up his own brewery in Lembeek, just outside of Brussels, and would be focusing on the tradition lambic beers of that region, Boon knew that it would be very hard to make a lambic blend and be profitable right away. (The price for a large bottle in 1975 was seventy-five cents per liter, and at one point this was the official price for lambic. It was the same price as three bottles of lager beer.) Pierre was, of course, more than happy to help spread the word about his Hoegaarden witbier beyond the town where it had been so far enjoyed.

Small breweries like Pierre's, especially those that produced beer often thought of as farmers' beer, were never taken seriously by the larger lager breweries in Europe. Beer that did not need to be filtered or required cooling facilities were considered dirt, or second-class beers from breweries that would soon close. Companies like InBev were able to undercut many small breweries, regardless of the type of beer they made, by giving discounts to customers, along with special incentives. Smaller brewers were not often able to sell their wares at the same price as the larger lager brewers, as no profit would be had. Pierre would sometimes sell his beer for the same amount as the lower-priced lagers but had no special conditions.

Boon would come to Hoegaarden and pick up bottles of Celis beer and deliver them to retail shops and cafés in Brussels. It was a hit. Though he was not the only one to distribute for Pierre, Boon had a similar passion for the beer as Pierre did. Pierre was always very welcoming and trusting of others, and when Boon would come to town, he merely walked into the brewery to get his bottles. Such was the trust Pierre had.

Boon describes this time as a new era for breweries in Belgium, which is saying a lot for a country whose national beverage is beer. The time was special, Boon says, as there were only a few of them starting out during the twenty-nine years after Pierre had started: Boon; Chris Bauweraerts of Brasserie d'Achouffe Brewing; and Pierre, who had started it all.

Before the Fire

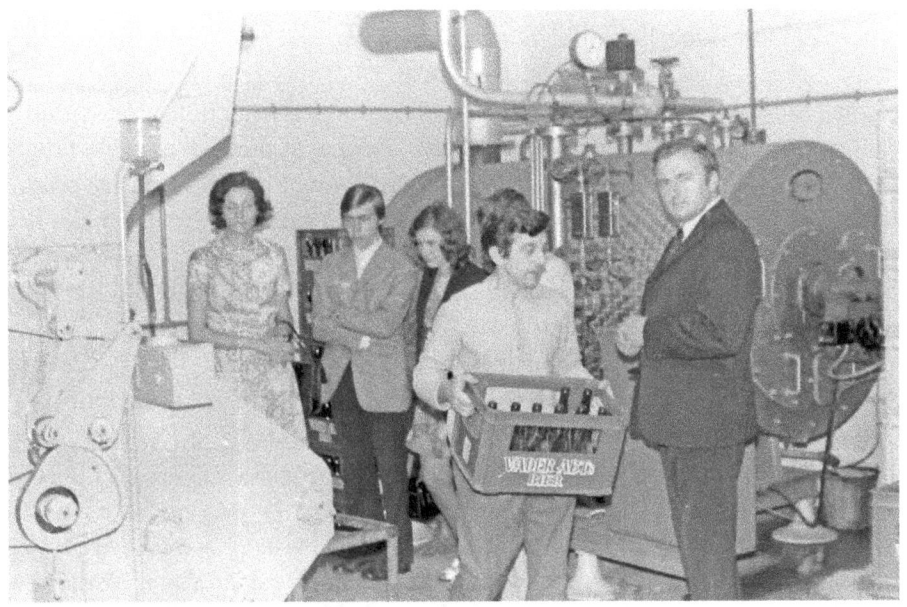

Pierre moving cases around the brewhouse, circa 1972. To Pierre's left is future Hoegaarden mayor Frans Huon. *Courtesy of Christine Celis.*

Pierre tightening valves at De Kluis around 1973. *Courtesy of Christine Celis.*

Recognizing that he could not make any meaningful profit on just the white beer, and wanting to experiment a bit in general, Pierre began to release other beer expressions. Besides the artistic satisfaction of stretching his brewers' legs, adding new beers to the lineup was tactical, as well. These new beers would be of even higher quality, allowing for a higher price point. If they were successful, Pierre would have a better opportunity to make his brewery successful.

With his brewery's reach expanding across Belgium and parts of Europe, releasing his take on other traditional Belgian styles would soon satisfy his growing number of fans. First up was a Gravinnebeer in 1969, a darker abbey-style beer that went well with the winters as much as the white beer did for the summers. The beer later became known as Vader Abt's Beer, or Father Abbot's, a clear homage to the abbeys themselves.

By 1972, though, Loriers would close, ending Pierre's regular source for yeast. Though he was outwardly calm, cool and collected, Pierre was actually quite distraught, unbeknownst to others. After all, where would he get his yeast now? The answer would lie with Mont Saint Gilbert brewery and its yeast. Though he had used that source at time when Loriers did not have any to spare, Mont Saint Gilbert was now his primary source.

Later, a mentee of Pierre's, Chris Bauweraerts, also obtained yeast from Raymond Moreau at Mont Saint Gilbert directly when starting his own brewery, Brasserie d'Achouffe, more than a decade later.

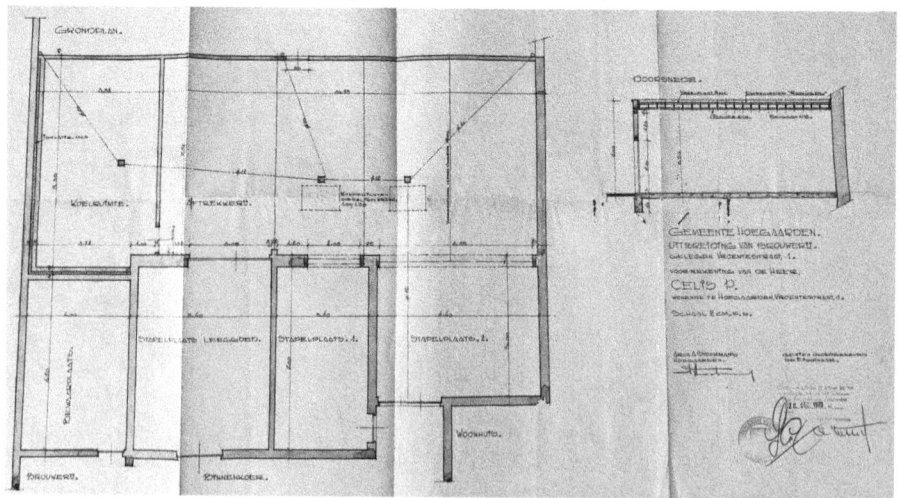

Pierre's expansion plans for the farmhouse brewery just four years after opening, December 28, 1970. *Courtesy of the author.*

Before the Fire

Pierre next to one of his copper kettles at the farmhouse brewery. *Courtesy of Christine Celis.*

Brasserie d'Achouffee founder (and Pierre Celis protégé) Chris Bauweraerts (*left*) and Pierre holding Pierre's first kettle. It was in this kettle that Pierre first practiced brewing his witbier in the early 1960s. *Courtesy of Chris Bauereraerts.*

Fun fact (as my sixteen-year-old would say) about the Mont Saint Gilbert yeast: It originates from the William Younger's Brewery in Edinburg, Scotland, which merged with the McEwan's Brewery in 1931, forming Scottish Breweries. In addition to Pierre and Achouffe's use of their strain, the mighty Duvel and Chimay Breweries also use yeast originating from Younger's/McEwan's Breweries.

Since breweries in Scotland often shared their yeast strains, the Edinburg yeast became a hodgepodge of different yeasts. Professor Jean De Clerck, a Belgian brewing scientist, made a "pure one yeast cell selection" of this combination of yeasts. De Clerck helped a multitude of breweries around the world in his lifetime, and when he passed away in 1978, the monks at the Abbey Chimay (yes, that Chimay) allowed De Clerck to be buried in their cemetery, making him the only civilian to have this honor. One could easily argue that the unique "Belgian character" we attribute to Belgian beers in the last one hundred years is due to De Clerck.

New Digs

By 1979, Pierre had outgrown the farmhouse brewery that housed Celis Brewery, and he needed to look for a larger facility. Pierre had hit seven thousand hectoliters and had no room to grow at the farmhouse. But he was still tied to the family farm that his brewery had called home for thirteen years. Every Celis business since Pierre's father moved the family in had been run out of the farmhouse.

Hoping to satisfy his need for a larger facility but keep his beer in Hoegaarden, Pierre looked no farther than a few blocks away. He had heard that the nearby Hougardia lemonade factory was available. Once a distillery as well, the building was perfect for Pierre's needs. Though he was tied to the name Brouwerij Celis, Pierre decided to rename the brewery when it moved into the former lemonade factory.

Now known as Brouwerij De Kluis (an attempt to identify with the monasteries of Belgium), the facility had a much larger brewing system, a larger bottling line and more staff. The new system included two 75-hectoliter (or 62.9 barrels) open fermenters. Much of this equipment came from other brewery closures, a fact not lost on Pierre. He also had the facilities to propagate his own yeast and no longer needed a supply from others.

Before the Fire

A postcard advertising the Hougardia lemonade factory, which would later become Brouwerij De Kluis after Pierre moved the brewery in 1979. *Courtesy of the author.*

Pierre standing next to one of his kettles at Brouwerij De Kluis. *Courtesy of Celis Brewing.*

Pierre had challenges revamping his new location, as the equipment that the former lemonade factory and distillery used for the juice and spirit needed to be moved for Pierre to modify the facility to his purposes. Acquaintances like Frank Boon helped Pierre with cooperage at the new facility, in addition to moving out the old lemonade equipment. Pierre supplemented some of these friendly helpers by employing those he saw around town who were not currently working. This not only helped Pierre with needed work but also allowed him to give back to his community.

During this time, Pierre's closest employees were two gentlemen named Beck and Maurice. Pierre relied on them heavily, though he still had the help of his old friend, mentor and advisor Marcel Thomas. Thomas worked with Pierre for years, but he never accepted pay from him. Both Maurice and Thomas were there on the first day of brewing at De Kluis, along with a few others, including Frank Boon. A few things needed to be modified, but on the whole, that first day went well for Pierre and company, save for one notable exception. One night before the first day of operations at De Kluis, thieves broke into the brewery, taking a few items, including the false bottom for the mash tun. It was not easily replaceable, and Pierre had to have the manufacturer make a new one. This delayed the first day of brewing, though from there it was smooth as silk.

Taking on a new location and expansion was not something Pierre could do on his own. Some outside investment was needed. The Winters family from the Holland region of the Netherlands reached out to Pierre. The family had made their money as bottlers of 7-Up and sold their shares to invest in De Kluis. Despite their lack of experience with the brewing world, they had a solid distribution network and the money to invest with Pierre. With this influx of capital, ownership of Celis was about fifty-fifty between Pierre and the Winters family.

The first couple of years for De Kluis did not see the profit all were hoping for. Though the need to make up the cost of expansion is something most businesses expect to happen, monetary losses the first couple of years were tough nonetheless. In fact, the capital disappeared at one point early on, forcing the Winterses to borrow more money. Pierre invested more as well. Finally, the tide began to turn at De Kluis.

In 1981, the village of Hoegaarden celebrated its one-thousandth year as a town. It was a momentous occasion, one that many towns never see. The following year, Pierre made his first trip to the United States. This was important—his love affair with the idea of America had been brewing for decades, and he was finally here. I doubt even Pierre grasped the effect that

Before the Fire

Pierre Celis and Christine at a Belgian exhibit in Washington, D.C. The pair are shaking hands with Prince (now King) Phillipe of Belgium. *Courtesy of Christine Celis.*

this first visit would eventually have. Pierre would not only take steps to bring his witbier from Hoegaarden to the United Sates (Texas was first up), but he also would help pave the way for Belgian products in general to come into the country.

To make brewery life a bit easier for himself and his employees, in 1984, Pierre decided he needed more space. He did not have to look any farther than the nearby Dumont farm on Stoopkensstraat, which was essentially next door to De Kluis. The facility allowed for increased production at a time when it was needed.

The Dumont farm was considered by many in the area to be of great historical value. The original owner, Jean-Baptist Dumont, was heavily involved with politics and was a brewer as well. Jean-Baptist Dumont built the farm in 1756 with his wife, Marie Vandermolen, the daughter of a town alderman and brewer. It would take marrying a brewer's daughter whose family had clout for Jean-Baptist to gain the credibility he needed. The well-known brook that Pierre and others used in later centuries for their breweries was the same one that provided Jean-Baptist with his brewing water. The farm was large, with three entry gates, stables and a barn, all made of natural stone. Expansions of the cellars and attic were made around 1831 and 1836.

Brouwerij De Kluis after the fire. *Courtesy of Christine Celis.*

Pierre's popularity in his native Belgium was clearly growing, as it was across the rest of Europe. Many were already copying the idea of the Belgian wit and producing their own variations. The Belgian breweries Brouwerij Riva, Brouwerij Van Honsenbrouck, Brouwerij Clarysse and Brasserie du Bocq each had their own take. Breweries in France and the Netherlands were also tinkering with their own examples.

To honor Pierre and his brewery, the side street off Stoopkensstraat, next to De Kluis, was renamed Hoegaarden White Avenue. De Kluis was employing around thirty-eight people at this time.

Before the Fire

Smoky and the Bandit

Pierre was also working on a side hustle or two at this time, the primary project being to produce a line of cave-aged beers. To this end, he purchased the Folx-les-Caves in 1985 (pronounced "Foo-leh-caves"). These caves were in underground limestone quarries in the Waals-Brabant region of Belgium. Pierre wanted to experiment with the brewing and aging process, so he intended to use the caves to age beer in a similar fashion as Champagne.

When Pierre formed a company (Folx-les-Caves SA) to handle his new venture, he brought on Thierry Fourie and Luc Vanderplas. Pierre contributed the caves to the new company, while Vanderplas and Fourier contributed their shares in cash.

All of the caves in the network, and the land above, comprised only three hectares, or less than a quarter of a mile. Pierre had wanted to see the effects of fermenting his beers in a cave and then fine-tune the aging process by handling it similar to how Champagne is handled in the bottle—that is, placing the finished bottles on a stand, letting the naturally occurring sediment in the bottle move around and turning each bottle a quarter turn after varying intervals of time.

If he was going to successfully pull off his idea, Pierre would need to visit wineries in the Champagne region of France to better learn the tradition of making this bubbly product. Now armed with the knowledge he and Luc needed, tests were performed.

The bottles he had in mind were seventy-five centiliters (roughly twenty-five fluid ounces), with a very sleek and slender shape. Once the roughly six-month aging process was complete, the cork would be ejected, a process Pierre had, oddly enough, tested with some of his beer in the freezer of his friend Vanddebosch, a baker on Doel Street in Hoegaarden.

Pierre felt that if the cave beers (as they came to be known) were successful, it would allow this project, as well as Hoegaarden itself, to become a haven for tourists. After all, the Folx-les-Caves were only seventeen kilometers (ten and a half miles) from Hoegaarden, with a constant temperature of twelve degrees Celsius. The temperature was as important for the fermentation and aging of the beer as was the turning of the bottles. To mimic the process with Champagne and to get the character he was striving for, the bottles (which sat on a rack) would need to be shifted a quarter turn periodically.

The De Kluis Brewery (which had converted the building next to it into a catering business) had already attracted a large number of tourists from around Belgium. Tours were arranged by café owners or clubs. Pierre saw the caves as a logical extension of his brewery, especially considering their historical value.

Pierre envisioned that patrons would start their day at the De Kluis Brewery then see a slideshow at the town hall, followed by a tour and tasting at the brewery itself. After the brewery experience, Pierre hoped to then take patrons on a tour of the Folx-les-Caves, rounding out their overall experience in Hoegaarden. He felt that the tour of both locations would allow visitors to experience what in his mind was a bit of what human evolution was all about. It is quite an interesting concept for a man who was thought to be concerned only with beer. For Pierre, though, the human condition involved much more. He knew that the beer would be unique, but what he was really looking for was the conversion of part of the caves to a museum of sorts.

"People of all ages will be able to watch the total geological development and the expansion of humanity. The proof is here for the taking: shells, shark teeth, elements that are the solid evidence that we came up to hear. I would like to make a representation of how man used to live in the ice age, how he sought protection against the climate by digging these holes with deer horn," says Pierre in *My Life*. "I would like to picture their way of living, century after century, in all these caves. But it would not become an amusement park, but an educational thing."

Twenty years prior to his purchase, Pierre had explored the underground caves. By Christmas 1985, he had completed an internal mapping, deciding then that this was what he had in mind for his cave beers. Few people knew the caves as well as Pierre; many could get lost without a guide.

The caves are a labyrinth of sorts, with many winding passages that are no taller than the average height of a person. During the Middle Ages, and throughout their history, the caves were used by many to hide in, the most famous being Pierre Colon, a well-known desperado in the late 1700s. Colon fell out of favor with local authorities after he either refused or was not able to pay his rent for the home he and his wife lived in. After the home (part of which borders the caves) was condemned, Colon and his wife were ordered to pack their belongings. They eventually stood trial. Colon later escaped and hid in the caves for about seven years, during which time he robbed passersby, redistributing much of what he pilfered to those less fortunate. Colon and his wife were caught again and executed in 1769. Not a pleasant fate for Belgium's own Robin Hood.

Pierre had gained an extensive knowledge of the caves over the years and found (with the help of a guide) the section of the caves that Colon had used as an apartment of sorts while hiding out. The "apartment" was nothing

Before the Fire

The entrance to the Faux-les-Caves, once used for the bandit Colon, later purchased by Pierre with plans to age his cave beer, or Grottenbier, in. *Courtesy of Christine Celis.*

more than a large hole with alcoves and exits in numerous directions. It was easy to see how the bandit evaded capture for so long. One such exit leads to a brook that locals referred to as the source of all life, including that of evil.

Pierre found that there was much graffiti on the cave wall, done by those who had visited over the centuries. A British soldier signed his name in 1919. That same year, a person named Gilot spent time in the caves and left his mark. Beer had even been brewed in the caves, and dances were led there by teenagers of the village. Even a TV series, *Johan en de Alverman*, was filmed within.

One can see why Pierre picked the caves for his project: the large amount of history. But his idea of using the Folx-les-Caves had to be tabled for the time being, as something else would occupy his time in 1985. In addition, the permits to modify the caves were stonewalled by the Wallonian government so that they could be used as a bat reserve. Instead, the little Belgian would later have his dreams of a cave beer realized in the caves at Kanne.

HERE COME THE BELGIANS!

Caves were not the only thing on Pierre's mind at this time. He had his eye on the United States, too. That year, he had been approached by Jim

Houchins and Bob Leggett of Austin, Texas, two Texans who had started Manneken-Brussels Imports, an importing company that focused on Belgian beers. The pair wanted to add Pierre's Hoegaarden Witbier to their lineup of Belgian imports that included Duvel Mortgaat and Chimay. Michael Tassin, a Belgian living in Austin, was Manneken-Brussels's liaison for Leggett and Houchins, having the advantage of speaking the language, as well as possessing a few connections.

The agreement was signed by both parties on January 1, 1984, in Belgium's capital of Brussels, and the contract would remain in force for five years, with automatic renewals every five years unless each party gave written notice within 180 days of the end of one of the five-year contract periods. The agreement allowed Manneken-Brussels to solicit orders from anywhere in the United States and to have exclusive import rights for De Kluis's beers in the nation.

Austin would greatly embrace not only the beers from Duvel and Chimay that Manneken-Brussels brought in, but also those of De Kluis. Pierre's Hoegaarden Witbier, as well as the Grand Cru, were immediately popular with beer fans. Local Belgian-friendly bars like Maggie Mae's and the ever-popular and infamous Gambrinus, owned and operated by Belgian ex pat Luc "BoBo" Van Mechelen, quickly carried and promoted Pierre's beers.

The agreement required De Kluis to participate in Manneken-Brussels promotional programs, including providing promotional materials, attending events as needed and ensuring that the quality of the beer imported was no different than the beer that remained in Europe.

Manneken-Brussels and De Kluis would share in the cost of any necessary state and federal licenses, though De Kluis would take the lead on obtaining them. If a conflict were to arise, it would be settled according to Belgian law, in the courts of Brussels.

Houchins, Legget and Tassin were excited to add Pierre's beers to their portfolio. For Houchins, it was like having a piece of his early adulthood (having attended school in Lueven, Belgium) in his own backyard in Texas.

After many discussions, an agreement was reached between the two parties, prompting Pierre to visit Austin later the same year. Pierre was immediately impressed. There was so much nightlife in Texas's capital city, and many people were open to trying new things, especially things from around the world. What helped solidify Pierre's impression of Austin was that the University of Texas was located there, providing a steady flow of potential new drinkers every year.

> HOEGAARDEN ENGLISH VERSION
>
> IMPORT AGREEMENT
>
> This agreement is made in Brussels, Belgium, this ___ day of ___, 1983, Brouwerij de Kluis whose address is Stoopkenstraat 46, 3320 Hoegaarden, Belgium, hereinafter referred to as the "BREWERY", hereby appoints MANNEKEN-BRUSSEL IMPORTS, Inc. whose address is P.O. Box 6366, Austin, Texas 78762, U.S.A., hereinafter referred to as the "IMPORTER" as the exclusive importer of its beers in the United States of America, its territories and possessions (the "TERRITORY") as follows:
>
> 1. The IMPORTER is authorized to solicit orders for Hoegaarden White and Grand Cru Beers (Ales) in the TERRITORY. It is understood that the importer shall have a right of preference with regard to an exclusive importation of the BREWERY's other products in the TERRITORY.
>
> 2. Prices for the BREWERY's products covered by this agreement are as set forth on the attached sheets, which are made a part of this agreement, and which are marked ANNEX A. Prices of the BREWERY's products may be changed by the BREWERY upon sixty (60) days' written notification, such changes to be effective sixty (60) days after the date of mailing notice of change to the IMPORTER.

A copy of the original import agreement between Brouwerij De Kluis and Manneken-Brussels Imports. This agreement is responsible for bringing Pierre and his beers into the United States for the first time, in Texas specifically. It was perhaps a sign of the future. *Courtesy of Jim Houchins.*

Christine Celis advised that adjustments be made to the labels of Pierre's beers to adhere to federal guidelines in the United States. Changes also included a more prominent display of the shield and staff from the original labels.

Over time, Tassin, who now worked for C.R. Goodman Distributing, began to be perceived as the main sales and marketing contact for Pierre despite not actually working for him. "There was a person who by that time had worked for Manneken Brussels, and who was then working with C.R. Goodman on their import company," says Chris Black, owner of Falling Rock Tap House in Denver, Colorado, who also worked at C.R. Goodman in the 1980s. "Michael was basically marketing himself as the face of the Celis brewery, like head of sales and the like. This is before the Austin brewery opened up."

One beer that required a mandatory label change would also be steeped in controversy: Forbidden Fruit. It was a stronger, dark Belgian ale that came in at a much higher ABV than the witbier. The label in Belgium featured a Rubens painting of Adam and Eve, with a beer glass substituted for the infamous apple. Although the image was popular in Pierre's native Belgium, the U.S. government had other thoughts, feeling that the nakedness of Adam and Eve was too risqué for Americans.

The Bureau of Alcohol, Tobacco and Firearms (ATF), precursor to today's Alcohol and Tobacco Tax and Trade Bureau (TTB), rejected Pierre's label for Forbidden Fruit for that reason. The government explained to Pierre that the label would be accepted if it was a work of art. Knowing its classic origins, Pierre went to the Rubens House in Antwerp, Belgium, for proof.

This seemed to satisfy the ATF, until it noticed that the apple in the painting had been replaced with a beer glass. Now considering it a forgery and thus no longer a work of art, it again rejected the label. Pierre was forced to add a little clothing to Adam and Eve to gain label approval.

Though Forbidden Fruit was now allowed into the United States under the modified label, some people were not satisfied with the prudish attitude of the government. Well-known international beer writer Michael Jackson decided to bring light to what had happened. Jackson, in an article titled "Forged" and featured in *Playboy* magazine, spent two pages telling the story of the original label. The article even featured a picture of it.

Per his agreement with Manneken-Brussels, Pierre would send the standard hexagonal witbier glasses and standard tulip glasses for the Grand Cru based on the number of cases of each beer sold. In addition, he sent promotional items, like cardboard cutouts and pamphlets, to the United States to help educate and promote. The cutouts featured background info on De Kluis, focusing on its Belgian roots, as well as on how to get the perfect pour of the witbier into the hexagonal glass. The ads were effective, making a personal connection between a brewery half a world away and its consumers in the United States.

Pierre made numerous trips to the United States to personally promote his beer. His daughter, Christine, often accompanied him. Christine was fond of many of the U.S. national parks and visited when she could. Ever the businessman, Pierre kept any eye on what he saw in local bars, breweries and restaurants with regards to beer trends on each of his visits.

At times in America, Pierre exhibited some of the "ask for forgiveness" attitude that worked well for him in Belgium. Chris Black described Pierre's craftiness. "I would occasionally have dinner with Pierre, because I had

Before the Fire

known him for years," says Black. "I was pouring beers at events that he was bringing in. One of the times was when it was still Hoegaarden and he hadn't left yet."

"We did a tasting of the beer in the backyard of the Ginger Man bar in Houston, and we smuggled the kegs there to the country. They basically put a layer of cases on the bottom of the pallet, put a keg on top of the layer and then built a wall around it and then put a layer on top as a cap and smuggled like four kegs into the country," says Black.

Pierre and Christine would attend beer festivals and conventions, always keeping some witbier and Grand Cru handy for promotion. Pierre even attended the coveted U.S. beer festival and competition known as the Great American Beer Festival, held in Denver, Colorado, each year.

Pierre's footprint in the brewing world was clearly growing. The first responses to the De Kluis witbier in Texas were better than expected. Though many wondered what this cloudy and dirty-looking beer from Belgium was, others overcame this initial response to a beer that was different from the perfectly clear adjunct lagers advertised to them by domestic brands like Miller, Coors and Anheuser-Busch.

The witbier of Hoegaarden was quickly seen as a flavorful and refreshing beer for the summer weather in the Lone Star State. Its popularity also helped to increase imports of other Belgian beers that had been in the country for a while, such as Duval, Chimay and St. Bernardus.

Though 1984 was a great year for Pierre and De Kluis, what 1985 had in store for Pierre was much more like what George Orwell had in mind when writing his iconic novel *1984*. Tragedy would strike De Kluis and forever change Pierre.

On October 7, 1986, Pierre and Juliette were on vacation in the United States. They were staying with friends from Hoegaarden who had moved to Atlanta, Georgia. The trip was to be a break for the couple. Then came a fateful call from Pierre's daughter, Christine, early in the morning. There had been a fire at the brewery in Hoegaarden.

Part II

AFTER THE FIRE

1986-92

A Major Setback and the Entrance of Interbrew

"My daughter Christine called me very early in the morning saying there had been a fire in the brewery," says Pierre Celis. "She only mentioned the office and the rest of that building, and she uttered some more words...until I realized that everything was gone."

The fire had started the previous night, around 1:30 a.m., in the dressing rooms and dining room near a high-voltage cabin in the area. The fire quickly spread to the brewery, engulfing it in flames. The timing was interesting. Earlier in the evening, one of Pierre's brewery engineers, Jan Van Gijsegem, had arrived to work at the brewery. Gijsegem lived in the town of Winnejem and commuted to Hoegaarden. Around 12:00 a.m., Gijsegem was conducting a routine tour of the buildings, which took around an hour. Nothing was out of place. An hour into inspections, he discovered the fire and called the fire department in the nearby town of Tienen, for Hoegaarden did not have one.

Pierre and Juliette wanted to quickly head back to Hoegaarden, and thanks to connections their host friend had, they were able to catch a flight later that day. Knowing the devastation that had befallen the brewery, friends had an ambulance ready for Pierre, as they thought he would faint at the sight of what had happened. As it was, many did not know how to

Firefighters rush to save what they can of Brouwerij De Kluis during the fire in 1985. *Courtesy of Celis Brewing.*

express their grief to Pierre. His own employees were shocked as well. When he arrived, Pierre had to ask them to start cleaning, as they were in so much shock. Hoegaarden authorities first needed to cordon off the area and do some cleaning to make it safe.

The fire department commander was a man named Beckers. He and his lieutenant, Ginckels, arrived on the scene with twenty-five firefighters. Within an hour, fire crews had the blaze under control. They had stopped the fire from affecting the fermentation tanks, storage room and the brewery room—these were safe and sound. However, everything was pitch-black, Pierre would later note. Most everything, from crates to insulation, were burned and still smoking a bit. The fire department commander investigated the cause and determined that it was not intentional, just an unfortunate catastrophe for the brewery. That was the extent of the good news. The fire had affected the bottling department, the storage room for beer crates, the lab and more. The brewery also lost two hundred thousand liters of beer.

By noon that day, the fire was gone, with only a few firemen injured. Some beer was left, and local papers announced that the town would be drinking the reserves, which were in a separate building and brought to friends in Merchtem to bottle. But what to do about cleanup, restoration and a return to brewing? Sure, the separate brewhouse was spared, but everything was covered in soot and was an utter mess. The citizens of Hoegaarden who devoured his beer, including his employees, came to Pierre's assistance. Roger Ausloos, who was a neighbor and employee, allowed Pierre to use his home for an office. Lab work was moved to Louvain-la-Nuevo, in Leuven, Belgium, to the northwest.

Fortunately, a decent amount of beer survived, having been kept in reserve tanks toward the back of the building in an area cordoned off from the rest of the building. The beer was loaded into trucks and taken to friends in Mertchtem for bottling.

Since it was not feasible to brew at De Kluis with the packaging hall destroyed, Pierre turned to Brouwerij Riva in the town of Dentergem. That facility would brew the entire De Kluis lineup and handle packaging as well. This allowed Pierre to keep beer on the shelves and his customers happy. He was able to maintain relations with distributors and café owners. Ever the savvy businessman, Pierre wanted to make sure that his recipe was safe from those who might wish to benefit from him. Christine Celis says that her father used a different yeast strain during this time.

Pierre also hired a Swiss company to handle the cleaning and restoration process. Not long after that was well underway, Pierre encountered a massive problem: he was underinsured. Pierre's insurance policy covered up to one million Belgian francs, but seven million was needed to rebuild. He needed investors.

Pierre hoped to be brewing within a few weeks but realized this would not be an easy goal to accomplish. Belgians without their beer are not to be trifled with. To speed up the time it would take to restore the brewery, Hoegaarden's mayor proclaimed that the contractors would work harder and have the teams increased in number. The remainder of Pierre's employees jumped into cleaning midweek. Assistance came from someone who would soon become a lifelong friend, Miel Mattheus.

Pierre met Miel in 1984, when Miel was a full-time teacher and local guide. The two hit it off, and Pierre insisted that Miel come work for him. "Pierre asked me to work for him and help with advertising. He wanted me to start right away," says Mattheus. "I asked how soon, and he said he wanted me to start the next day! I'm a teacher, I told him. I can't just stop."

Pierre also utilized the Dumont farm he had purchased a few years before the fire to help store and bottle the beer that had survived, as there was a lack of usable space in the brewery building that survived. The slope at the end of the Dumont farm was excavated to make room for the bottling unit behind it and a few other homes. Rows of pipes were installed that led from the De Kluis Brewery and the new bottling unit at the end of the Dumont farm.

The beer was stored for two weeks in warm rooms at Dumont; then, after bottling, they were stored for later transportation. A loading and unloading unit was put into place next to the Dumont farm, allowing all the brewery trucks to vacate the town streets. Dumont would also become home to the Kouterhof, a vaulted room used for receptions and meetings. Having the Kouterhof saved visitors from having to walk up the stairs at De Kluis as they had before the fire.

Other modifications were made to the aesthetics of the building. Cracks were repaired, and the existing vaults were reinforced. A souvenir shop was added, too. The brewing museum Pierre had wanted, however, never came to fruition. A local senior citizens group placed a statue of a small brewer in the courtyard of Dumont, prompting many to think it was in honor of Pierre. The statue remains in the courtyard to this day.

Despite the expansion with Dumont, Pierre would keep his Vroente brewing equipment at De Kluis, a promise he had previously made to the town. When the restored De Kluis officially reopened on September 20, 1986, Pierre could not help but remember that his great-grandfather once worked as a groom at the Dumont farm.

Pierre (*second from right*) and former Austin mayor Bruce Todd (*far left*), dedicating the ground-breaking of the Celis Brewery in 1991. *Courtesy of Christine Celis.*

After the Fire

Picking Up the Pieces

After the fire, Pierre called Miel to help find investors. Pierre still wanted him to join him at the brewery. Miel joined the team in 1985 and helped extensively with the cleanup and rebuilding. Pierre again got what he wanted. However, he also mentioned that bankers would become the majority shareholders in De Kluis. They wanted Pierre to stay on and handle day-to-day operations, except when he wasn't feeling well. When Pierre did become ill and was not at the brewery, the staff of the majority shareholders took over management of the brewery.

Pierre heard many a complaint from customers about the way things were being handled, prompting him to rely on loyal employees to help him keep tabs on the new management.

Eleven months after the fire, restoration of the brewery was complete. Pierre would take brewing of his beer back from Brouwerij Riva, and production resumed at De Kluis. To keep up confidence in the brewery, a local teacher, Achiel, who lived near the brewery, gave tours to visitors and reassured them that all was okay.

Miel Mathis was also in charge of spreading the good word of the De Kluis reopening, although he did much more. Much of his responsibility was to maintain the positive vibes about the Celis name that had been cultivated over the years. He also helped Pierre to keep up the spirits of the employees, who were dealing with internal challenges from their new investors. They had a lot to do—especially in the face of an unexpected rival.

This unexpected rival was not internal, like their new investors, however. It was none other than Brouwerij Riva, which began to brew its own witbier, Detergemse Wit. Well, it wasn't quite its own; the recipe was oddly familiar to many people. Though this was a clear violation of Riva's agreement, in grand Pierre fashion, he did not seek legal action, says Christine Celis. That was Pierre—forgiving to a fault.

Pierre tasked Mattheus with letting De Kluis fans, cafés and retail shops know that Pierre had returned to brewing his witbier at De Kluis and that the witbier at Brouwerij Riva was not his. He wanted no confusion in the marketplace.

Through connections at Stella Artois, Pierre obtained investment capital in his brewery that allowed him to rebuild. Stella would buy out the bankers who held majority ownership and let Pierre keep his shares. The company also asked him back to manage the brewery.

Stella invested what was needed to rebuild, allowing Pierre to remain in control. This ownership arrangement would not last long, as the Winters family sold 60 percent of its shares to the bank, which later sold them to Stella, making it the majority owner of De Kluis.

Not long after this new partnership began, Stella was bought by another rising brewing conglomerate, Interbrew. This new company would now be known as InBev. At this point, Pierre lost any control he had over the brewery he had worked so hard to build. Before Interbrew purchased Stella, Stella management was happy to let Pierre (who owned just under 50 percent at this point) to conduct business as usual. Pierre would be responsible for the employees and beer production and for maintaining prior relationships with vendors, cafés and others in the marketplace.

Another advantage of the Stella Artois money was expansion. "Celis went from neighbor to neighbor, handsomely purchasing farmland and a farmhouse. Celis used the farmland to expand his packaging line and built warm chambers where his bottles and kegs would undergo a secondary fermentation at a consistent temperature," says Gil Camps, Pierre's grandson. "The farmhouse, eventually called the Kouterhof, was used as a taproom that was attached to the brewery, giving Celis a direct line to serve beer to his community. The Kouterhof was the last stopping point for tours, which

Pierre, Juliette and a former Hoegaarden mayor at the grand reopening of Brouwerij De Kluis, post-fire. *Courtesy of Christine Celis.*

provided an extra revenue source as well. Additionally, what started with simple foods eventually expanded into a full menu. This enabled customers to pair his beers with classic Belgian-style lunch and dinner items."

By the mid-1980s, Pierre had almost twelve times the employees that he had in the mid-'70s. Christine says that by 1989, her father had around one hundred employees and was brewing around 300,000 hectoliters (251,600 barrels).

New Family Members

Around this time, someone who would later figure prominently in the Celis story entered the picture at De Kluis. In 1986, Pierre's daughter, Christine, met a young Hoegaardier named Peter Camps. Camps was a waiter at the restaurant Kouterhof when Christine first met him. His parents owned a furniture store.

Christine and Peter dated a while before they were married, and as the two became serious, Pierre asked Peter if he would be interested in working at the brewery. For Peter, it was a no-brainer, despite not having much knowledge of how beer was made. He was working at his parents' furniture store in addition to waiting tables.

Peter decided to give it a week to see how he would like the brewing life. If not, he would go back to working with his parents. Pierre had him start in the brewhouse, working with De Kluis's brewmaster as well as the shift brewers to master the mashing, boiling and fermentation processes. In all, Peter mentored with five brewmasters who had a combined 150 years of brewing experience.

In addition to the brewing process, Peter Camps learned other aspects of the business. He spent time in the cellars learning aging, and he did stints in bottling and canning plants and worked in shipping and sales. He typically worked five to six days a week.

Having started after the fire hit De Kluis, Peter Camps's experience with Pierre and his brewery was solely under the InBev ownership. Camps recalled what the environment was like at that time. "Initially it was good. They did not interfere too much. But at a fast pace they started to change things and the way they wanted to go at it," he said. "Their vision did not always match with Pierre's vision, so clashes start to happen. Gradually, he did less and less, then you come to a point where you don't want to show up anymore."

Celis Beer

Unexpected Challenges

Once Interbrew became involved and InBev was formed, management plans changed drastically. Pierre was still beloved by his fellow Hoegaardiers, however. At this point, all of Belgium and Europe knew of and loved Pierre Celis, and many breweries across the continent were emulating his famous wit. This was a problem by 1988. "Everyone in Europe was brewing a witbier. Even those in nearby Tienen, and all still loved Pierre and his beer," says Matheus. Even though these beers were a homage to Pierre, they were also competition. InBev soon felt that it could not effectively move on from the past with the specter of Pierre haunting it every day. InBev wanted to put its own stamp on witbier. It did not like the name Pierre Celis, and his legacy was becoming a thorn in the side of its progress.

Considered an annoyance now, Pierre was no longer valued. He would come to work most days and not be allowed to do much of anything, relegated to a desk half the time. He shared office space with Marc Boelens, who at one time had worked at the Haacht Brewery and came to De Kluis as commercial director. "At one point, Pierre just said he felt like a golden Buddha," said Luc Vanderplas, Pierre's close friend.

Brouwerij De Kluis, now referred to simply as the Hoegaarden Brewery, as it stands today. *Courtesy of the author.*

After the Fire

Pierre (*second from right*), Billy Forrster (*fourth from right*), Peter Camps (*far left*), Wayne Kleck (*second from left*) and De Kluis staff outside of De Kluis in 1989. *Courtesy of Christine Celis.*

Pierre felt more like a statue to be worshipped than someone running a brewery. InBev wanted to use him as the image of Hoegaarden while still brewing the beer in its own way. This would not work for Pierre. He no longer wanted to be just the face of his brewery; he wanted to run it, as his title, "president," indicated.

Pierre said the relationship with Boelens and the operations ran smoothly. Pierre wanted to buy the Loriers brewer buildings, which had been closed by Stella in 1973, for expansion, as they already had many rooms for an office and a brewhouse. Interbrew had placed José Dedeurwaerder in charge at Hoegaarden by this time, and he was not on board with buying Loriers. Despite this, Pierre says Boelens came with him for support, as an agreeable friend and coworker. They even kept in touch when Pierre later retired. Christine Celis remembered Boelens as a man who "likes to eat and drink."

Boelens would later take over running De Kluis after Pierre left, moving to the Stella office in Leuven to manage the Hoegaarden beers as well as other brands. Boelens would not last long at De Kluis, however; after two years, he died in a car accident outside of Leuven.

De Kluis employees gather with Pierre and Christine for a photo opportunity in late 1980s. *Courtesy of Christine Celis.*

By 1989, Pierre was sixty-four. Dedeurwaerder and others with InBev thought Pierre was beyond the age to continue with the brewery. But Pierre was not ready to retire. He accepted a buyout from InBev and began to make plans for another brewery.

Part III

TEXAS BOUND

1992–2001

I Will Go to Texas

Having retired from De Kluis, as well as having accepted the buyout from InBev in 1989, Pierre knew he was not done with the brewing world. It was his passion, one of his reasons for living. Pierre had been exporting several of his Hoegaarden beers to the United States since 1984 and had relationships with many people there. He wanted to pursue his longtime dream of having a brewery in the America.

Pierre had originally wanted to start a smaller home brewery that would be connected to a bar. However, a colleague with InBev talked him out of it. Vincent Brusslemans, the manager at Hoegaarden when Pierre left, told Pierre that a small brewery, such as he had planned, was too small for the quality of his beer. Brusslemans added that he wanted to partner with him in a new, much larger brewery. Brusslemans was a financially minded businessman, having worked at InBev as CEO.

Many familiar with parts of Pierre's story will tell you that Texas was always the plan for Pierre. Yes, Texas was the ultimate choice, but it wasn't Pierre's first consideration for a new brewery. Pierre had first set his sights on St. Augustine, Florida. He had noticed in previous travels that many people from around the United States spent their winters in Florida, which he saw as a built-in customer base.

During this time, Pierre played tourist, traveling all over the United States and talking about beer in every bar he went to, much as he did in the early days of Brouwerij Celis in Hoegaarden. He often heard folks talking about the larger breweries like Anheuser-Busch, Miller and Coors. He would visit small breweries based on recommendations, looking at what those new breweries were doing while contemplating his own upcoming venture.

"Sometimes, they gave me the name of a small brewer, but most of the time, the beer was not worth drinking," says Pierre in *Pierre Celis: My Life*. "Someone has an idea and money, he gets settled, and then he buys a book about beer brewing. Most of these initiatives fail." Pierre was clearly contemplating the potential success of his new project, wherever it happened.

Though Florida was an option, it was not one that Pierre seriously contemplated. "There were many people during the day," he says in *My Life*. "However, at nighttime they stayed indoors, and that is why I abandoned the project."

Though Texas was not his first choice, Pierre certainly did not think he was settling when he chose Austin as the location for the new brewery. In addition to getting to know a multitude of other residents around the country, Pierre had established friendships with his importers, Bob Leggett, Jim Houchins and Michel Tassin at Manneken-Brussels, as well as Luc "Bobo" Van Mechelen, who, along with his brothers, owned and operated a Belgian bar in Austin called Gambrinus. Van Mechelen's uncle owned a bar with the same name in Leuven, Belgium.

Another big help was Michel Tassin's aunt, Mrs. Peters, who was from Hauthem, Belgium, near Hoegaarden. She gave Pierre the hard sell on Austin as his next location. In choosing Texas of all places, it seems that Pierre was giving a message to InBev. Taking a page from the popular quote often attributed to Davy Crockett, Pierre was almost saying, "You may all go to hell, and I will go to Texas."

These Austin connections, along with the similarity of the water profile to that of Hoegaarden, the large student population at the University of Texas, the even larger cities of Dallas and Houston not far away and Pierre's realization that the people of Texas drank about the same amount of beer as those in Belgium, helped to convince him that Austin was where he should be. Pierre would still import his malt from Europe and his Saaz hops from the Czech Republic (American hops were too bitter for him). So, Austin's proximity to the port of Houston, where his supplies came in, seemed an additional selling point for the move.

Texas Bound

Pierre loved Austin and the American ability to embrace everything. But he recognized that the United States was very different than his native Hoegaarden. He felt it would take time to adapt to his new city. He was not used to Americans having less contact with their neighbors than Belgians did. Though Pierre adjusted and continued his love affair with Austin, he never made a permanent move to the Texas capital. He bought a house not far from computer giant Michael Dell, but only spent about half the year in the city. His daughter, Christine, and her husband, Peter Camps, occupied the home full-time with their children, Daytona and Gil.

Celis ultimately opted for a large-scale production brewery. But Pierre had at first wanted to start small with a modest brewpub, looking at Austin's Sixth Street as a likely location, where he might have the option to place his beer out in the market as well. However, his new partner, Vincent Brusselmans, had other ideas and ultimately convinced Pierre that a large production facility was the right way to go. Brusselmans reasoned that a large brewery would more easily lead to a possible future expansion. It would be better to go big now than spending more money later with building expansions. After all, Pierre was now in big-is-better Texas.

There had been one other option Pierre considered before deciding to build: buying up an existing brewery that had the capacity he was looking for, saving himself time and construction costs. In the late 1980s, the Spoetzl Brewery, Texas's oldest existing brewery and the maker of Shiner Bock, was up for sale for the first time in decades.

Before Pierre contacted Spoetzl to begin discussions on a possible purchase, he weighed his options with his future business partners and his family, as well as with Michel Tassin and Mannkekan Brussels, his longtime importer. It would eventually be on the advice of Tassin that Pierre would lean, and Tassin did not feel that the Spoetzl option was viable. Pierre decided against Spoetzl.

Vincent Brusselmans, along with fellow Belgian Jan Van Gijsegem, would form what in the United States would be called a venture capitalist company, Surongo, in 1990. Pierre Celis, along with Surongo, formed the Belgian Brewing Company, which served as the legal entity on paper that owned Pierre's new venture in Austin. Going back to his roots, Pierre named the new brewery Celis Brewery.

Pierre bought property at 2431 Forbes Drive, on the northeast side of Austin. He invested 55 percent of his own money into the venture, with Surongo investing 13 percent. Pierre also secured bank financing that made up the remaining 31 percent, giving Pierre the controlling ownership stake. He was back where he was meant to be, in control of his brewery's destiny. Local Austin businessman William Shea Jr. would serve as the brewery's engineer.

Construction began in 1991 with a great deal of excitement. Although home brewing had recently become popular in the capital city, Austin had not had an actual brewery since 1878. Residents were fascinated by this little Belgian who wanted to open a brewery in their city, and they were excited to have beer to call their own.

Pierre bought three copper kettles. Together with fermenters, serving tanks and like, Celis was operating a one-hundred-hectoliter brewhouse (or eighty barrels). Construction would take just under a year, and Celis Brewery officially opened to the public on July 11, 1992.

Kettles were not the only asset that Pierre brought with him from Belgium. He brought his old engineer, Jan Van Gijsegem, who helped with the construction and equipment. Once Celis was up and running, Van Gijsegem went back to Belgium. Peter Camps would handle many of the brewing duties, although Pierre did a lot of brewing himself.

Prior to the installation of the kettles, Pierre and his Belgian Brewing Company held a groundbreaking ceremony that was well attended by many prominent Austin residents and politicians, including Austin's mayor at the time, Bruce Todd.

Christine Celis notes that the brewhouse was designed in such a way that the kettles would be at the front of the building, with giant windows shaped in a V-like pattern allowing for an almost divine feel when lit up by the interior lights at night.

The entire brewhouse was designed in true Belgian fashion to utilize traditional Belgian brewing methods. To ensure his high standards for quality and consistency, Christine Celis says that Pierre installed a quality control lab, which gave him the ability to propagate his original, and proprietary, yeast strain. Kim Clarke, who would later become one of Celis's main brewers, came to work at the brewery in September 1992, straight out of college at the University of Texas with a degree in psychology, to work in the lab and assist with quality control. The bulk of her college degree centered on biology and chemistry classes.

"She played such an important role in the first brewery," says Christine. "She was the one that my dad really took under his arm. Kim did not have to run the operation. He could give Kim his vision, because she was really smart and she had a good palate, so my dad looked at her as someone who could do quality control, build the yeast and make sure the cells are healthy."

Texas Bound

Pierre's copper tanks brought in from Europe, being installed at the Celis Brewery in 1991. *Courtesy of Christine Celis.*

Celis Brewery
GRAND OPENING
Saturday, July 11, 1992

■ Open House / Brewery Tours ■

Saturday, July 11, 1992   1:00 p.m. - 5:00 p.m.
2431 Forbes Drive, Austin, TX 78754   (512) 835-0884

■ Reception ■

Austin Convention Center   6:00 p.m. - 12:00 a.m.
500 East 1st Street, Austin, TX 78746

Beer, soft drinks and buffet will be served. Cash bar for mixed drinks and wine
(■ Please no one under 21 years of age ■)
Invitation required at door for entry into reception & brewery

A pamphlet from the grand opening of Celis on July 11, 1992. *Courtesy of the author.*

With construction almost done on Pierre's Austin brewery in 1991, those beautiful copper kettles can be visibly seen. *Courtesy of Celis Brewing.*

A completed Celis sits stoic with its iconic copper kettles visible through the windows. *Courtesy of Christine Celis.*

Pierre with Marcel Thomas, inspecting the equipment at the new Celis in Austin, September 3, 1990. *Courtesy of Christine Celis.*

The copper kettle brewhouse of the first Celis Brewery in Austin, Texas. *Courtesy of Christine Celis.*

Clarke, who grew up in Vicksburg, Mississippi, before moving to Austin in 1986 for school, also had a family connection with the Celises. Pierre and Clarke's grandmother Anna Coventry (née Banherla) were childhood friends who grew up near each other in Belgium, Anna in nearby Tienen. She later moved to Austin. The family connections do not stop there. Clarke's great-aunt and Pierre's wife, Juliette, were friends.

Clarke's grandfather was a U.S. soldier who met her grandmother during World War II, married her and then brought her to the United States, where they eventually settled in Vicksburg. Her grandparents still spent a lot of time in Europe, keeping the family connection alive and well.

When Clarke arrived in Austin for school, her grandmother was already living there, so she moved in with her while attending classes. As a young teenager, she also learned the art of winemaking from her grandmother, leading to an interest in homebrewing before she was of age to legally drink.

Around the time she was graduating, Pierre's search for places around the country to open his brewery brought them together in Austin. Her grandmother served as Pierre's accountant for the first few years at the brewery. Pierre saw quite a lot of potential in Clarke, so much so that he sent her to Belgium for six weeks to learn from professors in the brewing program at Lovain-La-Neuve University in Leuven. Clarke also mentored under professors Jean-Luc Suys and Jan Vangysegem, as well as Bernadette Vanderhasselt.

Clarke was twenty-two years old when Pierre hired her. She reminded him of Vanderhasselt, who worked at his De Kluis brewery in Hoegaarden handling quality control. To Pierre, the female palate was much more refined than that of most men. He understood that women have more taste buds. As such, he was able to get more accurate feedback from Vanderhasselt, Clarke and other women in his employ when it came to flavor profile, off flavors and consistency in Celis beers.

Clarke handled a variety of roles at the brewery from the get-go, in addition to her work running the lab. She took gravity readings, bottled and brewed. "My very first day on the job, it was a packaging day of the very first batch of Celis White," says Clarke. "I was sitting there visually watching for high fills and low fills as the bottles were coming off the line."

In the beginning, Clarke would split her time between running the lab and brewing. Brewing did not occur every day. As time went on, and Celis expanded, Clarke was not only running the lab but also overseeing the brewing operations at Celis. "In the beginning we would have our brew days and our packaging days," says Clarke. "There was always something to do with the lab and quality assessments. It was an ongoing thing."

Texas Bound

Setting the Tone for the Future

Having the only brewery in Austin, Christine Celis says that Pierre had no real competitors. When Celis opened, Texas still had a few regional and smaller breweries. In San Antonio, Texas's oldest existing brewery, the Pearl Brewing Company, founded in 1886, was the largest beer producer in the state. San Antonio was also home to the second iteration of the Lone Star Brewing Company, also a large producer of beer in Texas. Spoetzl Brewing in Shiner, Texas, along with the Anheuser-Busch facility in Houston and the Miller Brewing facility in Fort Worth, accounted for additional brewing operations. But these larger regional breweries were not direct competitors to Celis.

About one month after Pierre broke ground in Austin, tragedy struck the fledgling brewery. Vincent Brusslemans, Pierre's partner, Celis Brewery president and avid supporter, died in a horrific horse-riding accident soon after Celis opened. Brusslemans's children inherited his shares, though Pierre would later buy out these shares. Though business continued, this would be the beginning of a string of unfortunate events to befall the Celis Brewery.

With Brusselmans's passing, Pierre's daughter took over as president of the Celis Brewery. Having already gained experience working with her father at De Kluis, Christine was well equipped to handle the growth of her father's new dream in Texas. As Pierre spent only six months out of the year in Austin, day-to-day business was handled by Christine, with all checking with Pierre having the final say. Decisions on the brewery's direction were handled by its board of directors, which included (as you can likely imagine), Pierre, Christine, Peter Camps and both members of Surongo, Belgian Jan Van Gijsegem and Brusslemans's heirs.

Pierre spent a good amount of his time making sure brewing production and internal operations were running smoothly. Though the daily happenings of his brewery were important to him, Pierre spent most of his time getting out among the people and doing what he did best: marketing himself and, by extension, his beer. He was not shy to let Austinites and Texans know that his was the better Belgian beer. It was authentic and brewed locally.

With his team in place, Pierre began beer production on March 19, 1992, prior to the actual opening on July 11, 1992. Up first to be brewed was, of course, his signature witbier. Dubbed Celis White, it featured the original witbier recipe from his Celis and De Kluis breweries in Hoegaarden. Being light in body and low in alcohol, it was an instant hit and perfect for the hot Texas summers, which seemingly last forever.

Residents of Austin were not the only ones curious about Pierre's new brewery in Texas. Belgian actor and director Wies Anderson came to Austin and filmed the first brew day at Celis for his television program the *Wies Anderson Show* and later sampled the first bottle. "Often they are just pretending in such programs, but Wies was actually present," said Pierre.

Though the opportunity to tweak the recipe of his witbier from its origins in Hoegaarden was ever present, Pierre did not take the "new town, new recipe" approach, and there was no real reason to. The beer was already popular thanks in part to the importation of his beer from Hoegaarden over the previous eight years. Those who had not yet had the pleasure of tasting it would soon become fans.

Local love of Celis White was not the only reason for its popularity. Pierre and his team at Celis took the opportunity to enter Celis White into several beer competitions, most notably the competition at the Great American Beer Festival (GABF) held in Denver, Colorado, and the World Beer Cup (WBC) held every two years during the Craft Brewers Conference (CBC). This proved to be a fortuitous decision.

In 1993 and 1998, Celis White took home gold medals at GABF in the only category the competition had close enough to the style, the Herb and Spice category. The Brewers Association, which runs both competitions, would eventually add more beer categories, including Belgian Style Ale. It was in 1994 that Celis White took home silver in that new category and then gold in 1995 and 1998, with Grand Cru taking silver in 1995. But Pierre was not done yet. At the WBC in 1996, he also took home bronze for the Celis White.

In addition to his attendance at GABF and the entry of his beers into the festival's competition, Pierre had reached out to the Association of Brewers in Boulder, Colorado, with the intention of meeting and getting to know many of the brewers in the United States. The Association of Brewers (AB) had been formed in 1983 and incorporated Charlie Papazian's American Homebrewers Association (AHA) with the intent to help the burgeoning movement of small and independent breweries opening up in the country at the time. In 2005, the Association of Brewers would combine with the Brewers Association of America to form what we now know as the Brewers Association.

Pierre visited Charlie Papazian's humble offices and spoke with him about the possibility of his joining the AB. According to Pierre, Papazian was shocked. "I told him I wanted to become a member. I took the man's breath away for I was only a small Belgian…and the first foreigner," Pierre writes in

Celis Pale Bock, Celis White, and Celis Golden Lager (now known as Celis Golden Pils) in the 1990s. *Courtesy of Christine Celis.*

My Life. Pierre did indeed join the AB and spoke fondly of the organization and its members, and Boulder in general, remarking that "everybody I met was very enthusiastic, and they constantly talked about flavors and successes and only occasionally losses."

It took some convincing for people to try the naturally cloudy beer, after brewers of American light lagers had marketed for decades that the cloudiness made for bad beer. Once this fear of a cloudy beer was overcome, Austin embraced it. Brewed at the same time at Celis was Pierre's Pale Bock, as well as a pilsner dubbed the Golden Lager.

Christine Celis notes that loyalty to his original witbier recipe, and the ABV notation on the U.S. labels, helped to prevent excise tax issues.

Starting off with familiar beers allowed Pierre to dial in his new system and ensure that the original recipes were up to snuff. This also gave Pierre and his team enough time to brew up enough of the White, Pale Bock and Golden Lager to stock the shelves of local grocery stores, bars and restaurants as soon as they opened. Both the White and Golden Lager were a great way to introduce drinkers to new beers without throwing too much at them. Just as the White was an approachable beer for those not used to new beers, Golden Lager was a nice alternative for those who enjoyed a macrobrewed adjunct lager, one that could easily compete with American favorites such as Budweiser, Miller and Coors.

Celis Beer

Christine Celis holds up bottles of Celis Pale Bock and Celis White in the late 1990s. *Courtesy of Celis Brewing.*

Christine Celis advises that soon Pale Bock comprised 48 percent of Celis Brewery's sales, with the White coming in at 16 percent and Golden Lager 14 percent in 1994. Pierre went with calling his amber ale Bock, as folks were familiar with the word from Spoetzl Brewing's Shiner Bock, and the TABC had advised Pierre that he could not use the term *ale*.

What of his original yeast strain? Well, Pierre had a plan for that, too. Pierre had brought his original yeast strain with him to Austin, in true Pierre fashion. "When we arrived in the United States," says Christine, "my father smuggled his yeast in vials that he had stuffed in his socks." That was Pierre, asking for forgiveness and not permission.

Additional growth for Pierre and Celis Brewery came from one of his most tried and true sources: himself. Pierre's greatest assets were his panache for new ideas and business, as well as his uncanny ability to connect with people. Through his travels in the United States, whether for business or competition, Pierre was almost always swarmed by fans or folks who had tried his beer at festivals like GABF, and he never turned anyone away. Pierre would always make time to talk beer with those who enjoyed the beverage. Consumers weren't the only ones who felt connected to Pierre. Retail outlets, bars and distributors loved Pierre's personal touch and down-home personality, too.

Texas Bound

The timing of Celis's opening in 1992 could not have been more fortuitous. That same year, Austin was becoming known worldwide for its live music, and this slid right into Pierre and Christine's desire to incorporate live music at the brewery. Over the next ten years, locals would gather en masse at Celis, vibing to local bands while imbibing Celis beers.

These connections are truly what helped Pierre spread the word of his beers and the Celis name. This led to an increase in sales and expansion outside Texas. Distributors around the country contacted Pierre to discuss the rights to distribute his beers. He almost never sought out contracts on his own.

First to get shipments of Celis beers was New Mexico in 1993, which Christine Celis says started with a chance encounter at GABF in 1992. Cases of Celis White, Pale Bock, Golden Lager and Grand Cru headed to the Land of Enchantment, with Pale Bock leading in sales.

A significant change in the beer laws of the Lone Star State took place in 1993. That year, the Texas legislature passed House Bill 1425, also known as the "brewpub law." Passage of the bill allowed for brewpubs, or restaurants that brew their own beer, to legally operate.

First up was Waterloo Brewing, owned by Billy Forrester, with head brewer Steve Anderson. It was followed almost immediately by the Bitter End, Copper Tank Brewing Company, Armadillo Brewing Company and the Stone House Brewery. Their arrival gave Pierre truly local competition, though the tiny Belgian never really looked at it that way. Pierre was glad to see more breweries in Austin and looked forward to the camaraderie that it would bring.

Until this point, Pierre's only local competition in Austin was the Spoetzl Brewery in Shiner, Texas, as well as Pearl and Lone Star Brewing in San Antonio, though Austinites considered Shiner as more of a local beer than those from San Antonio. Spoetzl, which also contract-brewed Pecan Street Lager for Austin native Davis Tucker, began to ramp up advertising in Austin as a means to extend its reach and compete with Celis. Upstart Hill Country Brewing, located near Austin, also arrived on the scene and became popular.

Not all shared in the camaraderie, though. In 1993, the Spoetzl Brewery, now under the ownership of the Gambrinus Company, wanted desperately to hang on to Austin's beer dollars, marketing its flagship Shiner Bock as Austin's very own beer, and not Celis or its Pale Bock, a clear competitor. It was a claim that Celis took issue with.

Wayne Cleck, communications director at the time, told the *Austin American-Statesman* that Celis beers were truly Austin. He pointed out that

Celis Beer

A delivery truck for Centex Beverages, displaying signage for Austin's first modern brewery. *Courtesy of Christine Celis.*

Celis beers are brewed and sold within Austin and are made using local water from the Edwards Aquifer.

In September 1993, Pierre also expanded into Europe, partnering with the De Smedt Brewery in Opwijk, Belgium, to produce Celis White and Celis Pale Bock after the brewery received an overwhelming number of requests for its beers in Belgium. Clearly, Pierre had not been forgotten. These Celis beers featured a longhorn cow on the label and Old West lettering and were distributed into the European market, including Italy, the Netherlands, Spain and France.

De Smedt brewed between fifteen thousand and seventeen thousand barrels during the first year for Europe, generating almost $5 million in sales. Celis beers sold well oversees, likely due in part to Pierre's Belgian origins and Europe's existing fondness for his beers when he owned the De Kluis Brewery.

Belgium in Austin

Though he was known for Celis White in Texas, Pierre's Grand Cru would eventually become his most popular beer. Though beer fans had been exposed to Belgian tripels from the likes of Duvel, Chimay and Pierre's previously imported Hoegaarden Grand Cru, Celis Grand Cru filled a gap, providing thirsty Texas beer fans with their own Belgian-style tripel brewed right there in Austin.

Recognizing that the American craft beer consumer also wanted new beers, Pierre was looking to add another offering to his lineup. This was satisfied with the introduction of Celis Raspberry in 1994. Another light-bodied, low-ABV beer, it was well received and more than quaffable in the hotter months.

By the end of the second year, barrel production at Celis Brewery had increased exponentially, with Celis now available in thirty states around the country. Celis was also looking at international distribution, with the possibility of moving into Europe and Asia. Initial production in 1992 saw 3,021 barrels of beer despite distributing only in Texas that year. By the end of 1994, Celis beers were available in multiple states, with production having increased to 11,667 barrels. Once again, Pierre's tenacity pulled out a winner.

Celis had the advantage of being perceived as a European beer, with all the quality that might imply, yet it was freshly brewed in Austin. This filled a niche, one that had been brewing with beer fans for more than a decade in Texas's capital city.

By 1995, the Celis Brewery had become so successful that the brewers began to experience challenges with meeting the demand from retail outlets, bars and restaurants. Pierre soon realized that he was going to need to expand if he were to keep up with this demand and honor his commitments. By this time, Pierre had a much larger majority ownership in his brewery, primarily because he had bought Vincent Brusselmans's shares upon his death a few years earlier.

Pierre had put a few feelers out to gain a perspective on what his options might be. To know you needed to expand was one thing; to have the capital was another. Pierre did not want bank loans. He needed a new investor, and Miller Brewing came calling in 1995, having already acquired 100 percent of longtime heritage brewery Leinenkugel's, located in Wisconsin, in 1988.

Miller Brewing's parent company, cigarette manufacturer Philip Morris—yes, that Phillip Morris—brought an offer of 85 percent to the table. Though Christine Celis says that her father did not want that high of a buy-in, Phillip Morris would not accept less that an 85 percent investment. Though this gave Miller/Philip Morris controlling majority, it did allow for Celis to use Miller's networks to move its beer into more venues.

Ever the pragmatist, Pierre discussed Miller's offer with Christine, son-in-law Peter Camps (who at this point had taken over all the brewing duties), industry friends and family. Internationally known beer writer Michael

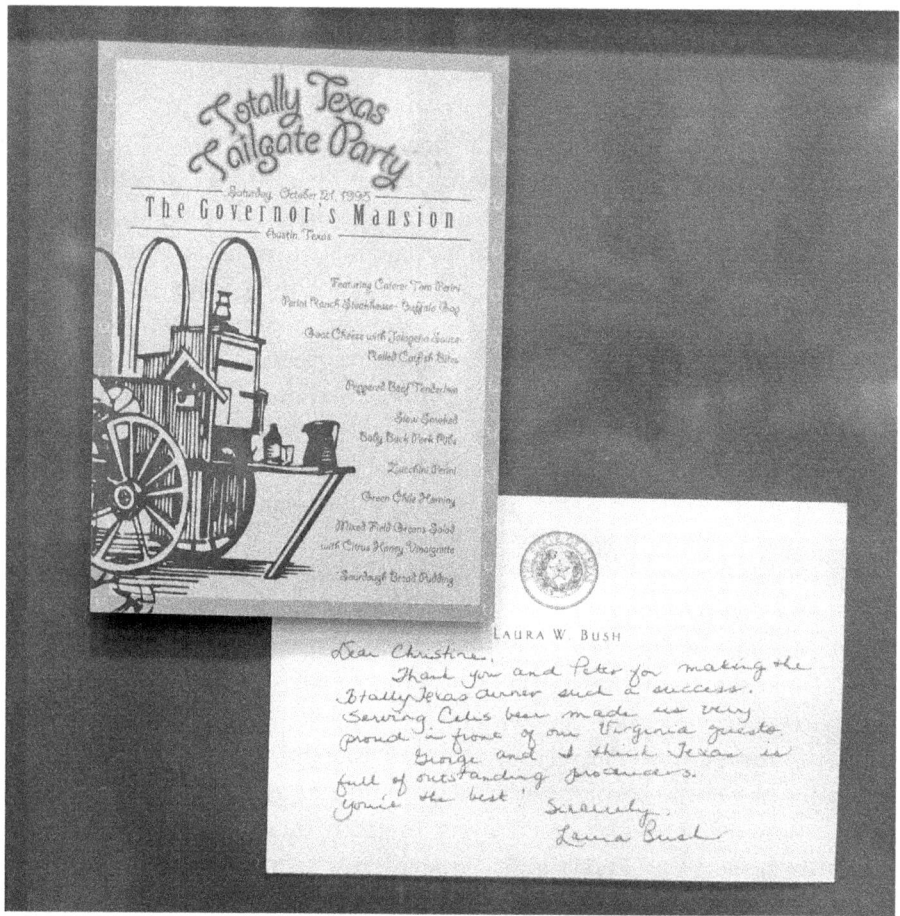

A letter from Laura Bush (First Lady of Texas) thanking Christine and Celis Brewery for providing a beer for her and Governor George W. Bush's private dinner with friends from Virginia, October 1995. *Courtesy of Christine Celis.*

Jackson was one of the industry friends with whom Pierre had discussed Miller's possible involvement. Jackson, who had written numerous books on beer, was not fond of the idea. Miller was a brewing behemoth and, though smaller than InBev, nonetheless exuded the common corporate philosophy of maximizing profit. It was less interested in maintaining quality and Celis's culture than in money.

A partnership with Miller would, in theory, be beneficial. With the number of small and independent breweries that were opening up by the mid-'90s, it was a way for Celis, considered a medium-sized brewery, to expand, stay competitive and take advantage of a lager distribution chain.

Miller sent Jacob Leinenkugel to sell Pierre on the benefits of jumping into bed with the brewing giant. Leinenkugel had stayed on at his family's brewery after Miller took over and wanted to reassure Pierre that a deal with Miller was a good decision. He told Pierre there would be no change to his brewery should he decide to finalize the partnership. Eventually, Pierre chose to partner with Miller. It was a pretty smart move on Miller's part to have someone who just went through a buyout to talk up the benefits to Pierre.

When it came time to let his employees know, Pierre was very positive about it, leading his people to become very excited about it. Despite the understandable apprehension of the unknown, most at Celis looked at the partnership as a positive. After all, it was a larger company coming in to help them expand, increase their tank space and give then nationwide distribution.

Jason Davis, now the Director of Brewing Operations at San Antonio's Freetail Brewing, worked at Celis from 1999 to 2001 as a brewer. He came to Celis during the days of Miller's influence. Though Pierre would always stop and give a word or two, Davis mostly worked with Clarke and Miller executives. Davis thought it was strange to see Phillip Morris as the name on his checks, but he learned laudable lessons on brewing a consistent beer.

During that first year, both entities worked well together. Miller let Celis do what it did best, and Celis was able to take advantage of a few things Miller had to offer. Miller helped with additional training for Clarke and others at Celis, sending them to Milwaukee for training in subjects like microbiology. At times, Miller personnel would come to Austin to administer sensory evaluation courses. "Everyone in the plant went through a program so that we could develop tasting panels to make sure that we were developing consistency," says Clarke. "For the equipment that we didn't have in the laboratory, we would send samples of the packaged product every month to Miller, and they would do a full analysis so we could evaluate trends in the product and make adjustments as needed."

This was the beginning of Miller's increased involvement in its new investment, though it would turn out that this was only part of the changes it would implement. Miller was skilled at consistently brewing the same beer over and over, but it lacked the small brewery's creativity. Miller did not seem to truly understand the value of Celis' beers, as they may have been too much of a specialty item for Miller to handle. Yes, they had been involved with Leinenkugel for many years before this, but Celis was more special and unique.

Many at Celis saw a lack of appreciation from Miller toward the consumers of Celis beers, with the company wondering why someone would choose a Celis White over a Miller Genuine Draft or Miller High Life. Celis was a small company compared to Miller, and though Miller went into the acquisition with the mindset of Celis becoming more successful, Celis was not going to be a priority.

As it was, at every point when Miller was going to implement a change, someone made an argument against it at Celis, whether it was Pierre, Christine, Clarke or Camps. No one just rolled over. Each made their voice heard. Though it can be beneficial to try new things and be open to what can be done better, there were instances in which changes at Celis were not so beneficial.

It was a struggle for both companies. Miller had difficulty understanding just what Celis was and what made the smaller brewery successful, as well as how to truly grow it. On the other end of the spectrum, Celis struggled with how someone could look at brewing only from an efficiency point of view and leave out the artistic side.

With help from Miller Brewing, Christine Celis said production brewing or forecasts for the brewery looked to have production rise to forty-five thousand barrels in 1996, though they did not achieve these projections.

As it was, Celis had seen 50 percent to 100 percent growth each year since the opening in 1992.

1992	*6,000 barrels (12,000 were originally projected)*
1993	*11,400 barrels*
1994	*15,000 barrels*
1995	*20,000 barrels*

This allowed for additional brewing equipment, as well as more brewery jobs. In another effort to reduce cost and focus on a core market, Miller pulled Celis beers from twenty-five states, with Miller keeping distribution to Illinois, Arizona, Georgia, Wisconsin and, of course, Texas. Christine Celis says Georgia was kept because, due to beer laws in the Peach State, brewers were not allowed to sever their relationships with distributors; and Wisconsin was of course Miller's headquarters.

New Jersey, being in proximity to New York, would have been another good choice, given its smaller geographic area, and it was not as densely populated with breweries as was California at the time. Without the precise 1995 data, it is difficult to say whether New Jersey or California would

The complete core lineup from the 1990s: Celis White, Celis Pale Bock, Celis Golden and Celis Grand Cru. *Courtesy of Christine Celis.*

have been better choices, but the data certainly points in that direction. It is important to note, however, that another reason for the choice of Wisconsin lay in the fact that it was Miller's home state at the time.

Now no longer spread thin, Celis was better able to meet demand on time and had, by this point, become the 46th-largest brewery in the United States out of 745 breweries overall that year, according to *Modern Brewery Age* magazine, moving Celis into the category of regional brewery.

With production increasing, 1996 saw a sixth beer added to Celis's portfolio, which was now being distributed in about two dozen states. Celis Raspberry used raspberry concentrate brought in from Belgium. The new beer was quickly embraced by Celis fans. Although fruited beers are hardly a novelty in Belgium, Celis did not yet have plans to release one. It had been fans of the brewery who requested it.

With Pierre still quite popular and revered in his native Belgium, it was natural to look to a brewing partner there to brew Celis White for Europe. Pierre turned to Brouwerij De Smet in Herzele, Belgium, though after it was acquired by AB InBev in 1999, Pierre looked to a new partner, which came in the form of Brouwerij Van Steenberge, known for such beers as Gulden Draak and Piraate and based in Evergem, Belgium. Though it operated from Pierre's recipe, using the original yeast strain and getting help from his old De Kluis brewmaster, Van Steenberge modified the recipe a bit, following a different process and ingredients. Van Steenberge used milled white wheat instead of Pierre's unmalted wheat.

In Stan Hieronymus's *Brewing with Wheat*, he quotes Jef Versele of Van Steenberge as saying that Van Steenberge did not want to brew a cloudy beer at first. "You do everything to avoid cloudiness," Versele said. "Cloudiness to my grandfather means infection."

In his book, Heironymus says that when Van Steenberge was brewing Celis White, they sold around 6,000 hectoliters (or 5,100 barrels) to thirty-five countries, mainly to Russia and Scandinavia. Celis's relationship with Brouwerij Van Steenberge would not last forever, though.

Around this time, Pierre renewed his Grottenbier (cave beer) project in the Folx-les-Caves. But he would soon run into challenges with the Wallonian authorities in Belgium. Due to the historic nature of the caves and the fact that they were also home to a large population of bats, authorities blocked Pierre from moving forward with his cave beer. In the end, Pierre sold the caves to them.

In 1997, Miller came to Pierre, Christine and Peter Camps with an idea to promote the brewery even further. It seems that longtime filmmaker and actor Clint Eastwood was looking for a brewery to partner with to produce a beer, with all proceeds going to various charities of his choosing. Miller connected Celis with Eastwood and his people to help develop the beer. There was a concept in mind of what the beer should be. Working with Eastwood and Miller, Pierre knew a final product would soon be revealed.

After taste tests at an event of Eastwood's at Carnegie Hall in New York, as well as one at a casting party for his film *Midnight in the Garden of Good and Evil*, Eastwood settled on the flavor he was looking for, with guidance from Celis. The next challenge would be the name.

Eastwood first wanted the beer to reflect his earlier Westerns, hoping for the name A Beer with No Name, after his iconic "Man with No Name" character in the Sergio Leone spaghetti Westerns. Many around him opted for Hog's Breath, after Eastwood's well-known restaurant in Carmel, California. Ultimately, Pale Rider was chosen in honor of his 1985 film of the same name, as the legal hurdles needed to clear the use of "Man with No Name" were not able to be overcome, and there were multiple bars in the United States with the name "Hog's Breath."

With an iconic image of gunfighters at the forefront of the label, the tag line "Proudly brewed for Clint Eastwood by his friends at Celis Brewery" was added, completing the imagery. All sales of the beer were donated to several charities of Eastwood's, including the Boys & Girls Club of Monterey County and the Carmel Youth Center. The beer debuted at Eastwood's Hog's Breath, with distribution to the rest of California and other western states.

The Celis team traveled to California for several events celebrating the launch, getting to see Eastwood, although the actor never made it to Austin himself for promotional events. These included Christine Celis and Peter Camps riding a stagecoach down Congress Avenue in downtown Austin. In 1999, Celis ceased production of the beer, as the "distributors didn't believe in it anymore, and there was no support from Eastwood," said Christine.

Pale Rider was hardly their only contract beer. Peter Camps notes that two years before, in 1997, Celis was approached by Lagniappe Brewing in New Orleans, Louisiana, to brew a series of its beers just for the New Orleans market. Celis and Miller took on the contract, though, by mid-1999, Miller terminated the contract due to low demand, lengthy fermentation time and minimal profit.

Celis had other special brewing projects. In 1998, in partnership with Texas A&M University in College Station, Celis brewed Aggie Bock, an amber ale that started with the Pale Bock base but was then tweaked a little.

The beer was marketed to A&M students and enjoyed modest success, though the beer would not last the year.

Not wanting to give up on gaining a good market share with the Celis brand, in 1999, Miller hatched the idea for Pierre Reserve, a beer that would be available only at the Paris Hotel in Las Vegas. Unlike Pale Rider and Aggie Bock, the Celis name was the only thing Celis about Pierre Reserve. Miller handled all the recipe formulation and production. By 2000, the beer had disappeared.

During this time, the relationship with Miller became less harmonious than ever. By the time 1997 came around, the honeymoon period between the two companies was over. Peter Camps recalls many conversations with Miller's technical directors in Milwaukee regarding ingredients used. Miller wanted to source from different vendors for the coriander and Curaçao oranges, as well as their wheat. At that time, Celis was locally sourcing its wheat for Celis White from Luckenbach, Texas. This weekly argument may not have helped Miller executives' view of Camps.

Celis' sourced ingredients were too expensive for Miller, which didn't put quality as a priority. They wanted the ingredients cheaper. Even the raspberry purée brought in from Belgium was switched to a cheaper, lower-quality version from one of Miller's vendors.

Miller began to ask Celis to cease using their Celis kegs and instead use kegs with "Miller Brewing Co." labeled on them. Pierre, Christine and Peter Camps were asked to take a lesser role in the active running of the brewery and instead travel more to promote the brewery. At this point, Pierre was getting more and more tired. Day-to-day running of the brewery was becoming taxing on the aging Belgian brewmaster. Taking advantage of that, Miller brought in its own person to take over brewing operations.

These changes were slowly and very subtly implemented by Miller. Pierre and company began to see multiple changes that would take place in the brewery while they were traveling to promote Celis. Despite having others in charge, there were many occasions in which Pierre, Christine and Peter were held accountable for decisions made by Miller. The decisions were not discussed with them in advance, according to Peter. Miller's response was always that the decision had to be made fast, so there wasn't enough time to contact them.

Another big change for Celis under Miller ownership was the departure of Peter Camps. In 1999, Christine Celis filed for divorce, prompting Miller to reconsider its relationship with Camps. When Miller's human resources department was notified of the impending divorce, it contacted Camps to advise him that he would no longer be part of the Celis family. "I was given 10 minutes to clean up my office," said Camps.

Over the next few years, Celis began to see growth slow to the point that sales were going down. By 1999, sales at Celis were down exponentially from the previous year. Miller then began to realize that maybe it did not know how to run a small, independent brewery that specialized in Belgian beer—a brewery that produced a product so very different from its own. In fact, Miller was having issues with its Shipyard brand as well. Miller didn't own 100 percent of either brand, but it did with Leinenkugel's, which the company wasn't having problems with, suggesting the problems stemmed from ownership stake.

That year, as the contract with Pierre and Cristine was up, Miller approached the father and daughter, offering to buy them out, as Miller did not wish to continue the relationship. This left Pierre and Christine with the only choice of selling their remaining 15 percent ownership, which they did in 2000. Miller would close Celis for good soon after in February 2001, selling most of the equipment and the Celis name to Michigan Brewing Company. Live Oak Brewing in Austin bought their kegs, and Houston's Saint Arnold Brewing bought a couple of the fermentation tanks, naming one of them after Pierre.

Pierre had made a legend of himself in the United States, specifically in Austin. Though many were a sucker for his Belgian accent, it was his ability to connect to people that won the loyalty of the masses. Even in Texas, he was referred to as the "Godfather of Witbier." Pierre's charm was known to all, and it was one of the bright spots for Jason Davis, who brewed at Celis from 1999 until the brewery's closing in 2001. "I did not get the chance to see Pierre too often," said Davis, "although I remember every time he was in the brewhouse, and he would greet us with encouraging words and a smile."

Part IV

THE IN-BETWEEN YEARS

2001–17

MICHIGAN BREWING

With Miller closing the brewery in February 2001, it would be easy to think our story has ended. If we have learned anything from Pierre, it is that he cannot sit still and always has an idea that he wants to hatch. "The doctor tells me I cannot save my body for my old age," said Celis one year after Miller closed Celis. "That is why I will work again with a vengeance. When I sit still, I am bound to die."

Pierre took some time off after the closure to gather himself. Though he was not pleased with the closing, he had no regrets from the experience, no bitter taste in his mouth. "If you analyze my life, America is the big finale," said Celis in *My Life* years later. "Texas is a nice place, and one feels at ease there. There are possibilities to make money and nature is well balanced. Can one ask for more?"

In late 2001, an opportunity came knocking for Pierre: a chance for the Celis beers of Austin to continue their production. Bobby Mason, owner and president of Michigan Brewing in Webberville, Michigan, came calling. A year earlier, Pierre's beloved copper kettles and brewing equipment were removed from the brewery and shipped off to Webberville. It was also the day he met Mason.

That year, Mason's Michigan Brewing Company had brewed 3,500 barrels of its own beer and began to break ground on a new facility that would be better able to accommodate the new Celis brewing equipment and tanks. The new brewery was completed in 2003. By then, Mason had already been brewing the Celis beers.

Bobby Mason was originally interested in buying Celis from Miller, lock, stock and barrel, intending to keep Celis in Austin. Mason was a little late, though, as Miller had already sold the building to local printers, Austin Printing Company. Not to be discouraged, Mason was able to talk Miller into selling him the equipment as well as the rights to the Celis name and labels.

Over the next year, Mason worked to get the equipment installed, and he was brought up to speed on the original Celis recipes, which Pierre and Christine said Miller changed to allow the use of less-expensive ingredients. Mason enlisted Pierre as a consultant to ensure he brewed the beers to his exact specifications, learning Belgian brewing techniques and the equipment. By early 2003, Michigan Brewing released its first batches of Celis, delivering them to Austin first and later Dallas, Houston and San Antonio. In that first year, Mason brewed between 501,000 barrels of Celis beers.

Almost three years after the closure of the brewery in Austin, Pierre embarked on his next project, the development of fruit beers that would be brewed in Brussels. Each beer in the series came in at around 3.5 percent ABV, an alcohol content common for the style, and were available in raspberry, peach and cherry.

With some Celis beers coming back to Austin and other states via Michigan Brewing Company, Austinites and others around the country had much to look forward to. Yes, Pierre and Christine were gone, but at least the beer was coming back.

Despite these successes, Mason had overextended himself with loans and with his investors, particularly his parents. By 2013, Michigan Brewing had closed and its assets sold, including Pierre's Austin brewing equipment and name.

Christine

After the closure of the brewery in Austin, Christine Celis took the opportunity for some much-needed downtime. Having not taken a vacation day in ten years, she bought a Harley and spent the next several years traveling around several states, taking time for herself. The break also gave her time to focus on her children, Daytona and Gill Camps, allowing her to spend more time with them than she had previously been able to. Her father's health was also beginning to decline, and she was able to spend more time with him.

By 2007, she went to work for Maura, a manufacturer of brewing, wine and cider-making equipment, as its sales agent in the United States. Christine stayed with Maura for the next year, traveling all over the country. It was during her travels to many breweries that the bug to have a brewery started to come back. Walking into breweries, seeing people handling different aspects of brew day and smelling the malt during mash-in and the aroma of the hops during the boil was all too much for her.

She also encountered person after person who told her they loved Celis beers or remembered visiting the brewery and meeting her dad. Their kind words served to reinforce the idea that re-opening Celis was what she needed to do.

While contemplating how to create a new brewery, she switched gears and went to work for Authentic Beverage Management (ABM), a beverage distributor and the sister company to Artisanal Imports, owned by Bob Leggett. Christine's focus with ABM lay with small Belgian breweries, many of which had never exported their beer to the United States before.

Since the Belgian breweries she was bringing in had different styles of beer, there was never an instance of competition between them while being handled by one importer. There was never an instance of having more than one brewery with the same style and having to make the decision about which one to push more. With ABM, she could help breweries that reminded her of the struggles her father had running a small brewery. She knew they could use any advantage to be successful. As many of the larger importers might pay attention to these breweries, it was her opportunity to give back. She knew the culture and what they were going through.

Eventually, Artisanal Imports decided to fold its ABM arm into the Artisanal umbrella. Suddenly, Christine had a huge portfolio to deal with, brands from all over the globe. It became an incredible amount of work for her and led to her losing some of her passion for the business. Not long after, in 2014, she resigned from ABM.

GROTTENBIER AND THE KANNE CAVES

During the period after his brewery closed, Pierre was still brewing his Grottenbier, or cave beer, in the Kanne Caves of Limburg, Belgium.

Label for Pierre's Grottenbier at the Kanne caves and a label for Celis White brewed in Belgium for European distribution. *Courtesy of the author.*

It was also around this time that Pierre took advantage of his previous relationship with the distributor Glazers and struck a deal for the import of the Grottenbier to the United States.

Though these were not the ancient Faux-les-Caves he had intended, the 100- to 150-year-old caves at Kanne did provide the right amount of humidity and steady temperature needed to produce the desired effect. Bottles were placed in racks called peters and turned every few hours for six weeks before they were ready.

The In-Between Years

Above: Pierre enjoying a bit of witbier out of his Grottenbier chalice around 2010. *Courtesy of Christine Celis.*

Left: Portrait of Pierre by Freddy Maanaerts, completed posthumously in 2015. *Courtesy of Christine Celis.*

Pierre, Luc Vanderplas and Luc's brother-in-law worked together to accomplish their project. Though their idea to use the history of Faux-les-Caves could be applied to the Kanne caves, they did take advantage of a very large portion of the cave, about a third of a mile from the entrance, as a sort of banquet hall for various festivities surrounding the beer, as well as for presentations on the process of making the Grottenbier. Shuttles were also available for visitors from the entrance to the caves to the banquet hall.

In the early 2000s, Pierre was all but done with his project in the Kanne caves. Declining health had much to do with the decision. By 2005, Pierre and Luc had sold the Grottenbier to fellow Belgian brewer St. Bernardus, well known to many for having once brewed the coveted Westvleteren Abbey beers as well as its own expressions. St. Bernardus brews the Grottenbier to this day.

The Giant of Flanders Passes On, Gypsy Beers, and Christine Tries to Get Her Name Back

By the late 2000s, Pierre's health had begun to take a turn. He had experienced a series of small strokes that left it difficult for the mighty Belgian to walk, let alone move. Pierre would sometimes experience bouts of vertigo, often making it seem as if his mobility was regressing over time. This frustrated Pierre, as one could imagine, for he was not able to run around as he often did in his youth or get in his car for a drive.

One later complication of his strokes resulted in blindness in one of his eyes, further complicating daily life. Eventually, complete blindness came to both eyes, making it difficult to tell the difference between night and day. He could not pick up a book and read, it was more difficult to eat; in some ways it felt as though life was stopping for him. He became more and more dependent on others. Though circumstances had changed for Pierre, one thing did not: his incomparable spirit and ability to smile to everyone. Pierre was saddened and worried, but he would not let this defeat him any more than other challenges in his life.

Pierre was still able to travel around the country, visiting breweries and connecting with people. One companion was Dally Vuletich, a New Zealand transplant who landed in Texas after a few years in Australia. "Dally the Kiwi," as he is often called, had met Pierre through Christine Celis. Dally often accompanied Pierre around the country, not just to keep an eye on

The In-Between Years

Pierre (*seated*), Juliette (*far left*) and Christine Celis (*second from left*), with a family friend around 2010. In this picture, Pierre has already lost his eyesight. *Courtesy of Christine Celis.*

him, but also as a close friend. Dally was always there to make sure Pierre was safe and taken care of, and his companionship allowed for a sense of normalcy for Pierre.

At this point it became too difficult for Juliette to take care of him at their home in Hoegaarden. Pierre was now in Belgium full-time and was moved to an assisted living facility at this point. Then, on April 16, 2011, Pierre moved on to that great brewery in the sky, joining the pantheon of Hoegaarden beer gods who had come before him, having forever changed the landscape of beer worldwide.

Pierre's funeral was quite the affair. In attendance were his wife, Juliette; his daughter, Christine; his grandchildren, Daytona and Gill; and others from outside Belgium as well. Frank Boon arrived in Hoegaarden, along with Chris Bauweraerts and what became known as the American delegation: Pete Slosberg and Rob Tod. They got together with Christine and family to celebrate the life of a man who deeply influenced everyone he met. It was an emotional time for all, one that would harden Christine's resolve to continue her father's legacy.

Pierre enjoying some sunshine on the bench outside of Dally's Down Under in Johnson City, Texas. *Courtesy of Christine Celis.*

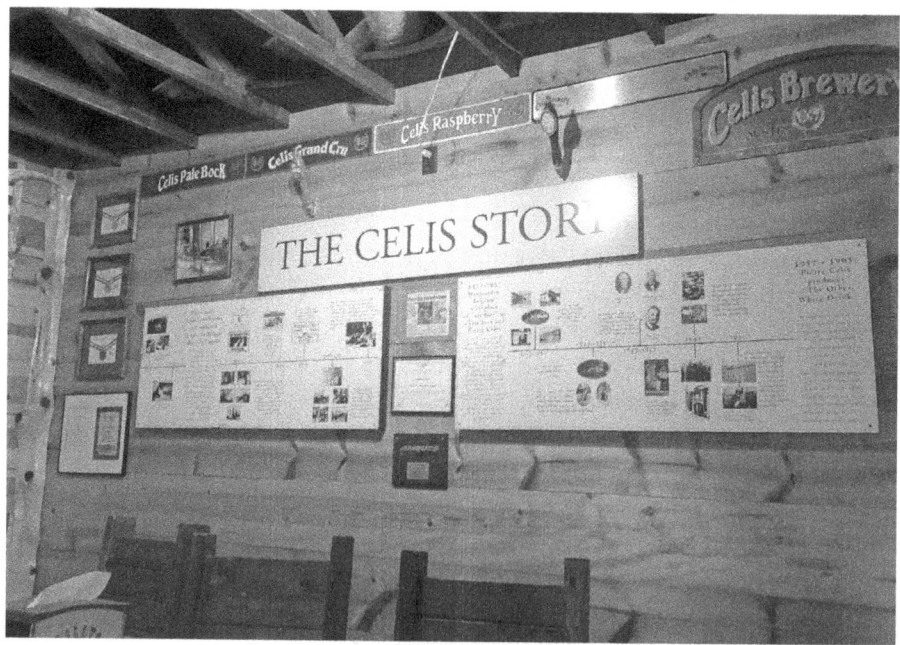

"The Celis Story" displayed prominently on one of the walls at Dally's Down Under saloon in Johnson City, Texas. *Courtesy of the author.*

The In-Between Years

Friends and family alike gathered for Pierre's funeral in 2011. *Pictured clockwise from top*: Rob Tod, Frank Boon, Chris Bauereraerts, Mil Es, Jean Luc Fuys, Robert Braekeleirs, Marta Arnauts, Christine Celis and Pete Slosberg. *Courtesy of Christine Celis.*

Over the next two years, Christine Celis knew that reopening her father's brewery was more important than ever, not just for her and her children, but also for his legacy. It was a no-brainer, but it would take time. In 2013, she planned a series of beers that would be brewed in collaboration with Austin-area breweries and would be released the following year. If it was successful, Christine planned to take the Gypsy series worldwide. The beers were also a means of getting the Celis name back into the forefront of the minds of Austin residents.

Each Gypsy beer would be a limited production, a decision Christine intentionally made. The idea was to honor a tradition among brewers from earlier times, when they traveled to make beer with other brewers. Often, only a small amount was brewed, and the beers were brewed only a couple of times.

Since a new Celis brewery would be a few years away, Christine wanted to keep the Celis name in the minds of beer drinkers.

The first collaboration was with Austin's Adelbert's Brewery, a Belgian-inspired brewery on the city's northwest side founded by Scott Hovey.

Looking to tie the Celis history with its future, Christine brought back former Celis brewer Kim Clarke, with whom she had stayed in touch since the brewery's closure in 2002.

Clarke created this first Gypsy recipe, a Belgian-inspired IPA, and, along with Hovey, worked through a few test batches before releasing it to the public.

Not long afterward, Christine was back at work on her Gypsy series, this time partnering with former Austin brewpub Uncle Billy's Brew & Que and Austin coffee shop Austin Java. Clarke was again tapped to work on the project, a key ingredient, according to Christine. "I will not do another Gypsy beer without her!" said Christine. The result was Dubbel Coffee Porter, a 7 percent porter that boasted cold-pressed fresh organic Peruvian and Guatemalan coffee, American malt and barley, as well as Belgian yeast.

Dubbel Coffee Porter was available around town at bars and restaurants on draft, as well as in four-packs of sixteen-ounce cans. The official launch took place at Uncle Billy's on November 7, 2016. Christine and Kim were in attendance, as was then-owner Rick Engel, Uncle Billy's then-brewer Brad Mortensen and Austin Java's roaster, Patrick Palmer.

Not long before she started the Gypsy collaboration beers, Christine began working on something that would be pivotal to her plans to reopen Celis Brewery: getting her name back.

When Michigan Brewing bought the Celis equipment and recipes, it also bought the Celis name itself. One hurdle to getting it back was removed when Michigan closed in 2012 due to severe financial trouble. Unfortunately, when Michigan Brewing closed, all of its assets went up for auction: equipment, materials and intellectual property, including the Celis name.

At the time, Christine was working with Craftbev International to get the Celis name back to Austin. Craftbev was already partnering with Christine on the groundwork for the new Celis launch, including solidifying the distribution network. Through Craftbev, she was able to get her name back, or so she thought. Craftbev and Christine differed on how to approach a new Celis. She wanted a brewery. Craftbev wanted to have the beer contract-brewed elsewhere. So, the partnership ended. Christine was not about to give up her father's recipes to someone else.

Not long after the acquisition of the Celis name and dissolution with Christine Celis, Craftbev sold the name to Total Beverage Solution (TBS), cutting Christine and the Celis family out of the deal and keeping the rights to the Celis name. TBS contracted with Two-Row Brewing in Massachusetts to brew the Celis White and Grand Cru.

Christine now had a dilemma, one that would not be quickly resolved.

Part V

MODERN TIMES

2017–PRESENT

The Road Back

Around 2014, Christine Celis began in earnest to reopen her father's brewery in Austin. Having already laid the groundwork with the Gypsy series of collaborations, Belgian IPA and Dubbel Coffee Porter, Celis was determined to get her father's brewery open.

Getting a new brewery off the ground would not be easy for Christine, for, although she had funds of her own to invest, she would need others, much like her father, to open the new Celis in the fashion that father and daughter would have wanted. To that end, Christine approached Atwater Brewing as a primary partner.

The partnership with Atwater would eventually not pan out, but Christine was not out of options. Tapping into her prior relationship with Uncle Billy's, she was able to get one of her first investors: Uncle Billy's owner, Rick Engel, in 2016. To invest in Celis, a production brewery, Engel would have to sell the Uncle Billy's intellectual property, as Texas does not allow for someone to own both a brewpub and a production brewery. Engel would bring in several other partners to invest.

Along with Engel, who had 25 perent, other investors came on board, including Bill Mulroy, who would later serve as Celis president and COO for about a year and a half. The combination of these individual investors would comprise 75 percent of the new Celis, leaving Christine with the remaining 25 percent.

For the moment, however, our story turns back to the issue of that nasty trademark of the Celis name. Not having the rights to her own name, Christine planned to reopen her father's brewery under the name Flemish Fox Brewery & Craftworks (FFBC Operations LLC). There was a purpose behind this name: "We speak Flemish, and Dad was a small, witty person just like a fox. He gets things done," says Christine.

Christine had made peace with this change, even though the idea of not having the Celis name ate away at her and daughter Daytona Camps. The equipment and her LLC were under FFBC, which was OK, but not for the name of the brewery itself.

Christine contacted TBS to discuss getting her name back. Although TBS refused her request, they did present her with a nice job opportunity with them, promoting the Celis brand. Christine ultimately turned down the opportunity, feeling that it would be too awkward to promote a brand that she no longer owned, one that would also be brewed on the East Coast with recipes not faithful to her father's.

Ultimately, TBS agreed to sell Christine the Celis brand back. TBS felt that that it was better for the Celis family to have the rights to their name. Money, of course, also played a part in its decision. Even if the beers were brewed under the Flemish Fox name, Christine would be brewing Pierre's original recipes, with the original names. Two-Row planned to brew under the Celis name but with recipes that Christine says had been altered several times over the years, starting with Miller and later Michigan Brewing.

A mere five months before opening, on February 7, 2017, Christine had her name back. The parent company would still be Flemish Fox, as all legal paperwork was in this name, but it would be doing business as the Celis Brewery.

Around this time, Christine was trying to get back her father's original brewing equipment from Celis 1.0 (the farmhouse equipment he started with in 1966). Historic though it was, just prior to 2017, no one seemed to want to preserve the equipment, much as Tomsin's equipment had been preserved in Bokrijk, Belgium. So, Christine sought to obtain the equipment and bring it to Austin, along with Pierre's foeders and a few fermentation tanks. The goal was to turn the building next door to Celis 3.0 into a living history museum—a place where visitors would not only learn about Pierre and the Celis family's history but also about Belgian brewing history and techniques.

Christine also needed a location for her brewery. The former Austin location for Celis wasn't even a thought for her. The building was now

Modern Times

On the left, Pierre's original mash tun from the Celis Brewery in Austin. On the right, the hot liquor tank at the Brouwerij Celis farmhouse brewery. *Courtesy of Celis Brewing.*

Pierre's original mash tun as it originally looked, now restored. *Courtesy of Celis Brewing.*

That taproom is gorgeous, isn't it? *Courtesy of the author.*

occupied and, as we all know, the former brewery's infrastructure and equipment were long gone. Christine would stick to the same side of Austin, however, and selected a twenty-two-thousand-square-foot building that once housed a flooring business in the industrial area of North Austin by Metric Boulevard and Rutland Drive.

Modern Times

Above: A far cry from the traditional copper kettles used by Celis over the decades, this modern brewing system is still very Belgian. *Courtesy of the author.*

Left: Celis fermentation tanks. *Courtesy of Celis Brewing.*

Christine was again working with Clarke and pulled together Pierre's original recipes. She contacted Katholieke Universiteit Leuven in Leuven, Belgium, which was storing and propagating her father's original strain.

"We have been working for years now to get the brewery back and under family ownership," said Christine. Remaining faithful to Pierre's vision, yet bringing Celis into the twenty-first century, Christine tapped brewer and industry consultant Bert Van Hecke to design her brewhouse and equipment. For Van Hecke, this was what he truly loved. "In my philosophy, it's all about personality," he says. "You don't just create a brewery; you create a personality."

Van Hecke cut his teeth in the Belgian beer world working as an intern with the likes of the famed Rodenbach Brewery in Roeselare, Belgium, and Trappist brewery Orval in Florentine, Belgium. After that, Van Hecke worked at Boon Brewery in Lembeek, Belgium, as its cellar master. He then moved to the renowned St. Bernardus Brewery, acting as its brewmaster.

Taking his expertise in another direction, Van Hecke also consults for breweries, fine-tuning recipes and diagnosing process problems. In addition to Celis Brewery, he designed a brewhouse in Franschhoek, South Africa.

Van Hecke wanted to round out his experience with training abroad. He worked with New Belgium Brewing in Fort Collins, Colorado; Brooklyn Brewing in Brooklyn, New York; Galati in Romania; and was brewmaster in Suzhou, China. With his reputation in the international beer world increasing, he has been asked to judge numerous beer competitions, including the World Beer Cup, the largest such competition in the world, held every two years during the Craft Brewers Conference in the United States.

These days, Van Hecke operates his own brewery in Roeselare, Belgium, under the name B.O.M. Brewery, which stands for "Belgian Original Maltbakery." Van Hecke wanted to have control over not only the brewing process but also his ingredients, when possible. Van Hecke hand-roasts his own malts, in traditional Belgian fashion, with a coffee roaster that he modified to work better with malts. Van Hecke uses white malt that has only been kilned and not yet roasted.

It was during her years as an importer that Christine first met Bert Van Hecke, so when it came time to ramp up plans for Celis 3.0, Christine turned to him to help design her brewhouse. One of the suggestions Van Hecke made to Christine was the recipe for Celis White. Since it had been modified so much after Miller took over, Van Hecke wanted a return to the original recipe.

That's a lot of Celis White, Pale Bock and Grand Cru. *Courtesy of Celis Brewing.*

To avoid any legal issues brewing Celis White, Van Heck suggested that Christine go back to the beginning and use her father's original recipe. This would avoid any entanglements. "This has been a long road," Christine said. "We have been working for years now to get the brewery back and under family ownership." Continuing her father's legacy was important to Christine and Daytona. "We have tried to be faithful to my father, while keeping an eye on what the industry has become," Christine said.

Celis would contract-brew beers for Uncle Billy's and Pedernales Brewing, which had once been located in Fredericksburg, Texas, but had been purchased by Bob Leggett. Also in contract-brewing arrangements were Lake Austin Ales and Viva San Antonio Brewing, which had connected with her at the San Antonio Beer Festival a few years earlier. In mid-2020, Celis also took over the contract to brew Austin-based Shotgun Seltzer's line of hard seltzers.

In looking at design, Christine had a few thoughts. One vision she had for the new taproom wasn't going to be as easy as one might think. She

Above: Found in Iowa a few years ago, this original kettle from the early Celis days in the 1990s in Austin was cut in half to act as part of the new taproom bar for Celis Brewery's current iteration. *Courtesy of Celis Brewing*.

Opposite: Pierre's granddaughter, Daytona Camps, stands proudly in front of some of her grandfather's original foeders (a large wood vat, or barrel, used for aging). Daytona brews at Celis to this day. *Courtesy of Celis Brewing*.

wanted to use the former kettles from her father's first Austin brewery as the centerpiece of a new taproom, recreating the bar from the first Austin-based Celis Brewery by using the Celis mash tun. She located two massive copper kettles: one in Ohio and another at a museum in Clarksdale, Arizona.

The Arizona museum was not willing to sell the kettle it had. But the kettle in Ohio was in a privately owned scrapyard, and the owner was only too open to sell it back to Christine. Once it arrived in Austin, the boil kettle was cut in half to create a circular bar reminiscent of Old World Europe, with taps and seating around the edges. It serves as quite the imposing image when one walks in.

Christine also raised funds to import the brewing equipment her father originally used in 1965 at the first Celis Brewery in Hoegaarden. Current plans also include a museum adjacent to the new Celis brewery that will house her father's original brewing equipment and other memorabilia. The equipment includes a four-thousand-ounce open mash tun, a coolship (a vessel for cooling beer), foeders (large wooden fermentation vessels), as well as her father's original copper kettles, which date to the 1800s. Through crowdfunding efforts, personal money and donations, Christine was able obtain most of the equipment.

The equipment now sits in a warehouse-style building next to the brewery that will house the museum. "We would like to have brewing classes on the original equipment, to teach once again the techniques used in the nineteenth century up to my father's time in the 1960s," she explains. Small-batch beers brewed on the equipment are planned and will be available only in the brewery taproom.

The project was placed on hold for a while, as Celis has had to shift focus to keep the brewery afloat in the face of the COVID-19 global pandemic. "We ramped back up our plans for the museum," Christine said. She added that they are actively restoring the old equipment and look to have the museum open later in 2021.

The museum is not the only project that fell a little behind schedule. Much like the first Celis brewery in Austin, plans are to have a large open-air stage in the space between the brewery and the museum. This, too, is now moving forward and is expected to open in time for the brewery's fourth anniversary in July 2021.

Something Old, Something New

Christine Celis, who once used roller skates to get around her father's old brewery, is modernizing this next chapter at Celis Brewery. "I remember being three years old, crawling into the open fermenters to help clean out the yeast," said Christine, who smiled as she remembered this time in her life.

Van Hecke brought in a 50-hectoliter (42.60 barrels) state-of-the-art automated brewing system, capable of turning out 43,000 barrels a year. The vision also included 100-barrel fermentation tanks, with a malting room on the second floor. When giving the manufacturer the details of what he was looking for, Van Hecke detailed everything, but in a way that the manufacturer would not know the logic behind his design, a philosophy that would extend to those hired at the brewery as well.

As funny as this sounds, it is very common in Belgium and Europe for brewers to leave out some details when it comes to equipment and recipes, allowing them to share information without giving away the farm, so to speak. It is not intended as a slight, merely a way to keep control over intellectual property.

Despite the newness of the equipment and the brewery, Van Hecke designed it to be very Belgian at the same time. That malting room on the second floor? "It was typical in Belgium to install the mill on the second floor, to create a gravity brewery," he says. "In this case, it was partially tradition, and also to save space inside the building."

The malting room was not the only creative design that also had a practical use. Unlike most breweries, Celis's hot-liquor tank (the vessel used to heat up the water for the brewing process) was located outside the building, not inside. Van Hecke says this was to save space inside the brewery, but it also allowed them to avoid higher temperatures inside the brewhouse.

Christine was also able to get her father's original yeast strain back. It had been stored in Belgium for propagation and safekeeping, allowing enough yeast to propagate by the new brewery's opening.

The next piece of the puzzle was determining who would head up brewing. Christine wanted Kim Clarke to stay on, but Clarke had established a career in the pharmaceutical industry since leaving Celis and was not in a position to leave just yet. Clarke today consults from time to time for the new Celis Brewery. Celis brought on former Rahr and Sons' brewer Craig Mycoskie as head brewer, allowing the resurrected Celis Brewery to start off with someone who brought with him a wealth of brewing industry experience; Mycoskie would depart a year later.

Initially, Christine and company brewed the well-known Pale Bock, an East Coast–style IPA, with the famous Celis White, Grand Cru and others following shortly thereafter. Celis opened for business on July 11, 2017, twenty-five years to the day when Celis 2.0 opened in Austin in 1992. Beers were first available in stores, though brewing operations had begun months earlier in 2017.

Daytona Camps, who had recently returned from continuing her brewing training in Belgium, rounded out the brewing team at Celis. Camps developed a love of her family's history and brewing when she was nineteen, after her grandfather Pierre's death. Looking for direction, Camps realized that her grandfather's extreme passion for brewing had now become hers as well. Initially, she brewed at an Austin-area brewery for two years. She then left Austin and guest-brewed around the United States and Europe, gaining

Left: Past meets present. 1990s Celis Grand Cru, next to present-day Celis Grand Cru. *Courtesy of Celis Brewery.*

Right: O.G. Celis fans were clearly stoked for the return of their original craft brewery in 2017. *Courtesy of the author.*

more experience. One such internship was with Old First Ward, a brewpub in Buffalo, New York. Now back in Austin, Daytona continues the Celis tradition as the third generation of brewers in her family.

Despite Celis's popularity among newer beer drinkers and elation from 1990s Celis fans, 2019 would prove an enormous challenge for Christine and her brewery. A very ambitious distribution plan and sales goals implemented early on by the board of FFBC led to more debt than all involved thought would happen. Despite 320 percent growth in 2018, money owed on loans, build-out of the brewery and a desire by the board to have a quick return on its investment proved too challenging for FFBC.

By early 2019, many of FFBC's individual investors declined to put any more money into the brewery, not confident that it would help to satisfy the mounting debt let alone get the return on investment they desired. "The brewery has struggled to make financial ends meet under larger than expected debt service since day one. Even though our beer has been one of the fastest growing craft beers in Texas, the financial model we started with put us in a cash crunch that simply did not give us any room to maneuver in a highly competitive market," explained Christine. "We intend to fix all of that through the Chapter 11 process. It will allow us to continue to make my Dad's legendary beers and grow within more realistic parameters."

In the June 21, 2019 edition of the *Austin American-Statesman*, a public sale notice was published indicating that Celis, or FFBC, would be put up for auction—lock, stock and barrel. The sale of the building and later the equipment was intended to satisfy a lien placed by Amplify Credit Union, one of FFBC's major debtors, whose loan had been used to help start the brewery.

Though prematurely called, the demise of Celis 3.0 would soon be stalled when Christine and the FFBC board filed for Chapter 11 bankruptcy protection, allowing them ninety days to reorganize their debt and company structure. "Everyone was able to keep their jobs, and we were able to continue brewing beer to supply our retail accounts and taproom," said Christine. "We have several interested parties as far as potential new investors."

Over the course of the next few months, Christine and the FFBC talked with three key groups interested in not just contributing to the brewery but also to buy it outright, though they ultimately pulled out. Eventually, it would be a local Austin group that bought FFBC, ensuring that beer would continue to be brewed at Celis. As a condition of the sale, Christine had to give up the intellectual property of her family name and divest herself of an ownership stake in the brewery.

Christine and Daytona, as well as many brewery employees, were able to keep their jobs. This was an advantage for Celis, as it allowed the new ownership to not only keep Celis family members on the team but also keep the beer's consistency and quality. Christine now focuses on sales and marketing and remains the face of the brewery, while Daytona has taken on a more significant role in brewing operations, helping to create new beers like the Violet Crown Quadruple Ale.

During the Chapter 11 process, no changes were made to the beers Celis was brewing—neither the ingredients nor the recipes. The core brands of Celis White, Pale Bock, Grand Cru and the popular Juicy IPA continued.

Celis received a great deal of support from industry partners. Distributors like Brown Distributing, which handles distribution of Celis beers in the greater Austin area, were ecstatic. "Brown Distributing extends our congratulations to our partner, Celis Brewery. We have remained vigilant amid all the conjecture and had full confidence that Celis would continue to flourish in Austin. We are extremely proud to be a part of bringing this iconic local brand back to Austin and have been overwhelmed by the consumer and retail support. Cheers to endless years!" said Brown in a statement released soon after the Chapter 11 filing.

Left: The beauty that is a Pale Bock being poured, truly a sight to behold. *Courtesy of Celis Brewery*.

Below: White, White, White. *Courtesy of Celis Brewing*.

Modern Times

Beer and car fans alike show up to Celis for one of its many hot-rod shows. *Courtesy of Celis Brewing.*

Although brewing contracts with Uncle Billy's, Pedernales, Robert Earl Keen and Lake Austin Ales ended while Celis restructured, Celis later picked up new contracts. Buffalo Bayou Brewing Company out of Houston needed someone to help with brewing capacity while it finished construction on its new and larger facility. Celis fit the bill perfectly. San Antonio upstart Viva! San Antonio Brewery also tapped Celis for production of its beers while it finalized plans for its first brewhouse.

The reboot of Celis has hardly been all doom and gloom, however. Since reopening in 2017, Celis has introduced a number of small-batch offerings as well as a couple of new year-round beers. At the beginning, we saw the introduction of Juicy IPA, a West Coast–style IPA, a mango-infused hazy IPA called Mango Maximus, a lime-infused Berliner Weisse–style beer and the Dubbel Coffee Porter. There have also been Black Currant Berliner, Hop Shuvit, Tangerine Maximus, the Leige Stout, a Belgian Waffle Stout, Weisenburger Festbier, Märzen Amber lager and the return of Pierre's Golden Lager, now known as Golden Pilsner.

In the years since reopening, Celis has continued such community events as the Punk Bock Festival, celebrating the release of its bock-style beer of the same name. The event included numerous local Austin punk bands such as Chromagnus, Splif, Chris Toast and the Jerks, Zero Percent and Worm Suicide. The event, including a potluck-style food element, was dubbed Punksgiving.

Left: A Celis employee pours an Oktoberfest during the 2019 Oktoberfest party. *Courtesy of Celis Brewing.*

Below: One of the Celis Brewery's new offerings, Juicy India Pale Ale. It is quite different from Pierre's offerings in the 1990s or his offerings in Belgium, but it is definitely in the spirit of his willingness to adapt to the market. *Courtesy of Celis Brewery.*

Opposite: Poster for the release of Punk Bock in 2018. Local Austin punk bands joined in for the fun. *Courtesy of the author.*

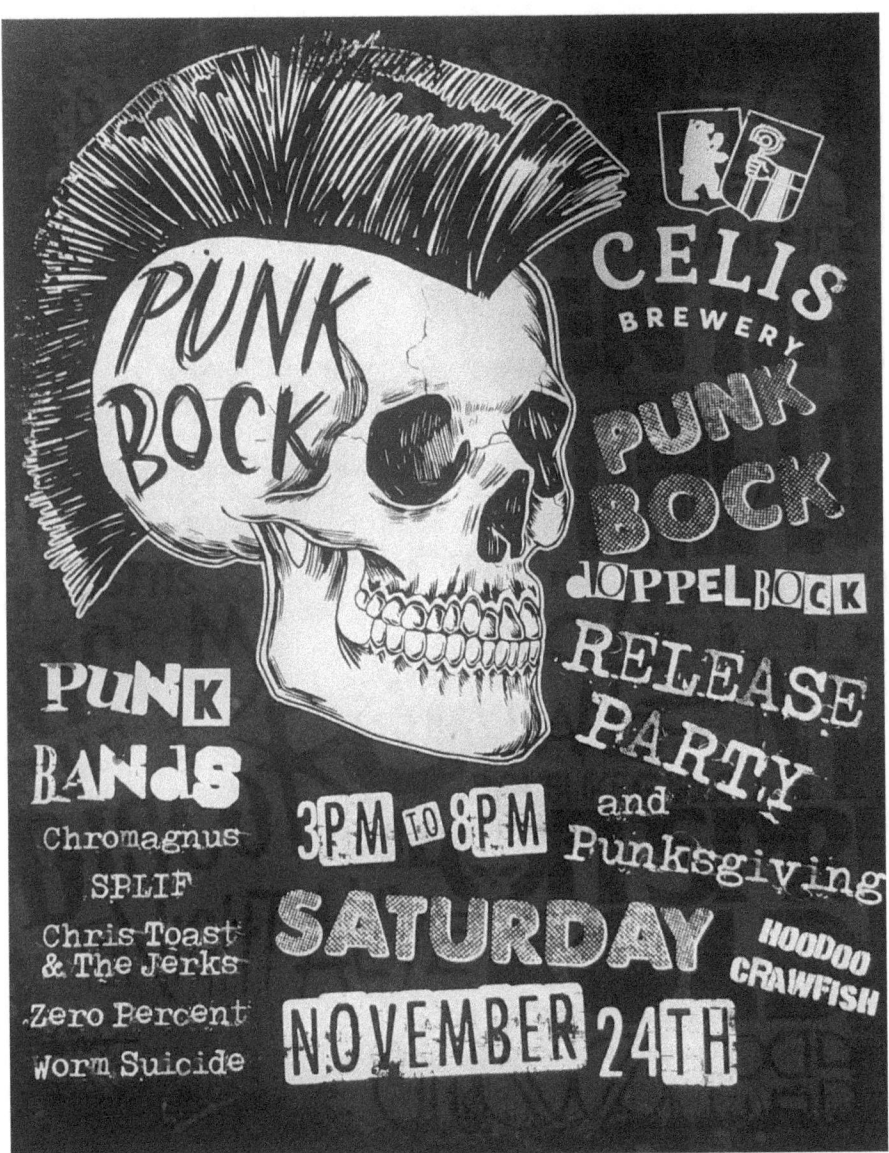

When fall arrives, Celis holds its own Oktoberfest celebration. (Yes, Celis knows it is a Belgian-style brewery. But remember, Belgians are all about the beer.) Unlike many breweries, Celis does not release only the märzen-style beer popular historically for Oktoberfest, but also a wheat-forward festbier, a style more commonly seen during Oktoberfest celebrations in Germany and Munich specifically.

The wall of witbier, with a little skateboarding and punk rock tossed in. *Courtesy of Celis Brewery.*

Weekly events include BYOV (Bring Your Vinyl) Night, when thirsty beer fans can connect with each other over good beer and a shared love for the only way music should be listened to; Wags and Waffles, an event for the community with good old-fashioned Belgian waffles and man's best friend; Geeks Who Drink trivia night; Beers and Bingo nights; games nights, which include board games, card games, video games and puzzles; multiple-themed live music nights; Super Bowl viewings; sponsored events at retail partners around town, like Chicken Sh*t Bingo; Blues and Booze; and even a burlesque performance from local troop the Jigglewatts Burlesque Revue.

One of the more popular events is the annual celebration of Pierre's birthday. Balloons, streamers, cake and more are brought out each year in

Modern Times

The bear and staff, the Celis family crest and shield, representative of Celis both past and present. The bear represents strength, honor and protection. The staff is the traditional shield and staff of Hoegaarden and represents the village's wealth, importance and royalty. *Courtesy of Celis Brewing.*

celebration of the dearly departed brewer, along with one or two small-batch special releases. It is a tradition carried over from Celis 2.0 in the 1990s.

During the COVID-19 pandemic in 2020, Celis canned water for its employees, to assist with a distribution network caught off-guard by the pandemic that caused a run on bottled water at most grocery stores. But that wasn't all the brewery did. With its taproom closed for a couple of months, Celis, like many breweries, worked hard to keep its name out there. Celis hosted numerous online happy hours, as well as an online concert series featuring Texas music. These actions kept existing and new fans connected to the brewery, allowing a smoother transition when the taproom was allowed to reopen.

By March 2020, despite surviving the Chapter 11 reorganization, Celis needed a new director of operations. The answer was brewing industry veteran James Hudec, who had a bit of a history with the Celis family. "It's a really good fit for both of us," says Hudec, whose exposure to anything Celis began in 1994, when he was apprenticing at Hill Country Brewing. Hudec would often stop by Celis after work to pick up beer and got to know the staff at the time. Sometimes, Pierre would be there. The staff would often give Hudec low-fill bottles or kegs that he would take back to his above-garage apartment at Southwestern University in nearby Georgetown.

Crowds gather at the celebration of Pierre's birthday at Celis in 1995. *Courtesy of Christine Celis.*

It was in 1994, at a beer festival at Sundance Square in Fort Worth, that Hudec got to know Pierre and Christine. "I remember meeting this short little guy with curly hair and this funny accent talking about Belgian beers," says Hudec, who, not long after, took an unexpected opportunity to apprentice-brew with Hausbrauerei Altstadthof in Nuremberg, Germany.

Hudec had a homebrewing system in his garage, making primarily ales, which he would serve to his neighbors, along with any beer he got from Celis. At the time, Hudec was a music major at Southwestern and planned to work in the music business and did not plan on a career as a brewer. However, it was a chance meeting with his roommate Nicky's father, who was from Germany, that changed his career path. Nicky's father tried some of Hudec's beer and was impressed. When Nicky's grandfather returned to Germany, he mentioned Hudec to his friend Dr. Ernsperger, who owned a brewery in Nuremberg.

By this time, Hudec had graduated from Southwestern and was looking for a job. He received a call from Dr. Ernsperger, who asked Hudec if he would like a one-year internship at his brewery. Months later, Hudec was brewing in Germany and would stay for two years.

The festival in Fort Worth would not be Hudec's last encounter with Pierre. Just before he was to leave Germany and head back to Texas, Hudec

Left: Happy patrons enjoy Celis beer around the copper kettle bar in the present brewery's taproom. *Courtesy of Celis Brewing.*

Below: An artist's rendition of the soon-to-be-finished beer garden and music venue. *Courtesy of Celis Brewery.*

contacted Pierre. Pierre was in Hoegaarden at the time and was happy to meet with Hudec, even giving him accommodations at his home (he stayed in Christine's old bedroom) while he was visiting Belgium. The two would talk beer for hours and travel around to breweries with Pierre as tour guide.

By 2003, Hudec was looking to start his own brewery in Brenham, Texas, though he would later travel back to Belgium and again visit a bit with Pierre. Hudec had kept in contact over the years with the Celis family. One of these interactions with the Celis family happened while Hudec was heading up brewing operations for Alamo Beer in San Antonio, prior to heading to Baltimore. Hudec wanted a Belgian-style wit on tap and designed one based on his recollection of Celis White. To make sure he got it right, he consulted with Christine Celis, who filled in the gaps. Hudec was also instrumental in locating the equipment from Celis 2.0 for Christine. "I was traveling through Arizona when I came upon one of the kettles," says Hudec. Christine was not able to purchase the kettle and get it back to Austin. The other kettle was in Iowa and much easier to acquire, becoming the centerpiece of the new taproom.

So, it was not a stretch in early 2020 for Hudec to start work at the new Celis. A project that he was working on as part owner in Baltimore had recently fallen through. Hudec and his wife were looking to relocate to Texas, specifically the Austin area, where they had been so many years before. Hudec called up Christine, looking for any information on possible openings at other breweries for brewmasters, specifically contacts at Dixie Brewing in New Orleans, Louisiana.

After explaining the situation to Christine, she told him he should come to work with her, running the brewing side of the operation. Though Hudec had never worked with the Celis family directly, the relationship was already there, and he started work in March 2020. Hudec's brewing team now consists of Nikko Stephen (who worked in various capacities at Celis in the 1990s) and, of course, Daytona Camps.

PIERRE'S LEGACY

Long before Christine Celis brought her father's brewery back, and at the same time making it her own, many persons in the brewing world were influenced by Pierre, taking elements from his beers and stories when opening their own breweries. Though it's easy to say that brewers in Belgium and Europe were heavily influenced by him, those in Texas and Austin were as well. The list of brewers and breweries affected by Pierre is endless: Chris Bauweraerts of Brasseries d'Achouffe; Pol Ghekiere of Interpol Brewery in Houffalize, Belgium; Rob Tod of Allagash; Tim Schwartz of Bitter End and Real Ale; and Brad Farbstein of Real Ale.

As with many others, Pierre served as a major inspiration for a young Brad Farbstein, who was just getting his feet wet with brewing and looking to open his own brewery "I used to go on the tours at Celis in the early '90s," says Farbstein. "I went so many times, that at one point I was told not to come back, unless I was going to bring someone new with me."

Farbstein would soon realize his dream, when, in 1997, he purchased a very small fledgling brewery in Blanco, Texas. Farbstein has grown Real Ale exponentially since then, but one of his biggest highlights occurred in the winter of 2005, when Pierre and Christine Celis attended a holiday party at Real Ale. "I had come to know Christine, and by default her father, over the previous years," says Farbstein. "I patterned my Real Ale

The author takes a break enjoying a witbier from the Interpol Brewery in Houffalize, Belgium, on a bench outside at the brewery known as "Pierre's bench." Pierre was fond of the witbier here, and his name is carved in the backing to the right of the author. *Courtesy of Sean Elfstrom.*

A better view of "Pierre's Bench" at Interpol Brewery. *Courtesy of the author.*

White after Pierre's Celis White." Plans were also in the works at the time for Farbstein to contract-brew beers for Pierre and Christine, though this never came to fruition.

Others still counted Pierre and Christine as major influences, including Kevin Brand of (512) Brewing, and the list goes on and on. To capture everyone who was mildly or heavily influenced by Pierre would take almost a volume in itself. It is impossible even after reading this book to truly grasp his importance and that of his family.

All of this influence comes from a man who started out in the family cattle business and then reinvented it as a dairy farm, and then, in his forties, scrapped everything to pursue something he truly loved—everyone else be damned. Pierre was going to do things how he wanted, and whether anyone believed in him or not, he was going to be successful. Pierre loved everyone and everything. Everyone was his friend and his brother. He never turned down helping his friends, both new and old. Many times, this love of humanity was to his detriment, and he was horribly taken advantage of, though this never discouraged him.

Modern Times

Pierre knew that anything is possible if you put your mind to it, and he was determined to let everyone he came into contact with know this. It is a spirit that was passed on not only to his wife but also to his daughter and his grandchildren. The Celis name has at times come and then gone. One thing is certain, though: not a decade goes by when you don't hear it, or even drink it—in the form of beers from all over the world. These days, almost every brewery imaginable has a Belgian-style witbier, all because Pierre refused to let anyone stop him from spreading his passion.

Much like a phoenix rising from the ashes, Celis is reborn. The brewery is back, and with it a grand brewing tradition from a family passionate about beer and protecting history. After all, Pierre was right when he said the "beer makes friendships." Rock on, Pierre. Rock on.

Appendix I

BELGIAN WITBIER

A HISTORICAL PERSPECTIVE WITH A FOCUS ON HOEGAARDEN BEER

Yvan De Baets, Head Brewer/Owner,
Brasserie de la Senne, Brussels, Belgium.

Origin and Context

The Hoegaarden beer, revived by Pierre Celis in 1966, is one of the three classic styles of beers brewed in and around the city of Leuven (Louvain in French), in the region of Brabant in what is now Belgium. It takes its name from the village it was brewed in: Hoegaarden, located thirty-two kilometers southeast of Leuven. Leuven used to be a major brewing center from the fifteenth century, as was Brussels, the other big city of the Brabant region. The two cities have been in competition for political and economic power for many centuries. Their growing populations and the ease of finding quality grains suitable for brewing in their surroundings have helped them develop their brewing industry over time.

The Hoegaarden beer belongs to the family of the white beers ("witbier" in Dutch, "bière Blanche" in French), the speciality of the region. That category took its name from their pale, white-ish and cloudy aspect. They belong to the broader family of wheat beers, as wheat imparted a big part of their typical character. Wheat was widely used

Appendix I

in Belgian brewing in the past, but not in the amount found in white beers, where it was a minimum 30 to 35 percent of the grist, often more. They were running beers (in opposition to keeping beers, like lambic or saison), in the sense that they had a very short shelf life and had to be drunk quickly (within a few weeks) in order not to deteriorate. Their origin can be traced to the fifteenth century; some claim their recipe was invented by monks.

Three different major types of white beers were made: the Leuvens Wit ("Blanche or Bière de Louvain" in French), the Peeterman (sometimes written "Peterman") and the Hoegaarden. Those beers had a great success in Belgium from the late fifteenth century until World War I. The Louvain and the Hoegaarden were considered among the important Belgian classics. They were extremely popular, meaning their reputations exceeded their local areas and they were known in the entire country. They were indeed "exported," which at the time meant not that they crossed borders, but that they were sold in other cities. As an example, as early as 1513, Hoegaarden exported 78,000 liters of beer to...Leuven. At the very end of the eighteenth century, the village exported 3,250,000 liters to the (then) Austrian Netherlands. Their fame also had as a consequence that they were imitated in other parts of the country, which has been the case for the Louvain, but probably not for the Hoegaarden.

Hoegaarden, now a mid-size village, at the time a small town surrounded by fields, was in itself an important brewing center and could build a reputation that attracted brewers from abroad. It might seem strange, as it was not even a real city. The reason, as is often the case, lies in politics and, hence, in taxation. For many centuries, the village, an enclave located at the border of the Duchy of Brabant and the Bishopric of Liège (another important, independent and powerful region of the time), the latter of which it belonged to, could evade supervision by any authority, avoid taxes and, more generally, avoid rules regarding beer brewing. It is easy to understand why so many people decided to open a brewery there (thirty-eight in 1758, for a population of roughly two thousand inhabitants).

In 1560, the brewers created a guild that had the reputation of being very rich and powerful. Hoegaarden belonging to the Prince-Bishop of Liège, all the brewers were obliged to be officially Catholic and swear fidelity to the bishop and his successors. The sons of the local brewmasters had the right to become brewers at their turn, but those who weren't from a family of local brewers had to pay an "entry fee"

Appendix I

to be part of the guild and prove that they had been in the trade for at least twelve years. The quality of the beer was controlled, and the bad ones were confiscated. The competition among brewers was strictly regulated. Many a brewer became mayor of the town. The beer was also made in the nearby smaller villages but not very far abroad. Surprisingly, Hoegaarden also had vineyards, but it seems that its wines have always been surpassed by its beers.

The brewers were most of the time farmers as well. Those farms clearly had a certain importance and wealth, as they were equipped with a (small) brewery. Around 1900, the average size of a brew was twenty hectoliters (seventeen barrels). Some of those beautiful Brabant-style big square farms are still seen today. The beer was served to the workers of the farm and sold to local people, later to taverns and cafés. Some breweries without a farm existed, but it was rare.

All the breweries were located along a very small river crossing the village in the south. They were taking their water from it, and it was said that a real Hoegaards beer could only be brewed with that very water.

Only indigenous cereals were used, but around 1900, the farmers had opted for new hybrids, which were easier to grow. Hops were also locally cultivated, mostly by private persons, but they were gradually replaced by hops from abroad (mainly from the region of Aalst, near Brussels).

Around 1870, about sixty-five thousand hectoliters of beer were brewed in the village, in fourteen remaining breweries. Their number was still the same right before World War I. At the turn of the century, some farmer-brewers were sharing a brewery. Each of them—helped by their team—was brewing at their turn, then brought the beer in the cellars of their own farm. That practice had been common in the town since brewing started there.

During World War I, the production of wheat beer stopped, as wheat was kept for making bread. This has actually been the case during every war shortage in the nation's history. After the war, the customers were seeking other sorts of beers (lagers, or stronger barley-only, top-fermented beers en vogue at the time). Those beers were then drunk locally only before slowly disappearing. The last brewery of Hoegaarden, the Tomsin Brewery, closed its doors in 1957.

Appendix I

General Characteristics of the Belgian White Beers

Summer Running Beers

Except in their region of origin, where they were drunk all year long, these beers were especially drunk during the summer for their refreshing proprieties. Their shelf life was very short, from one to two weeks for a Hoegaarden in the summer to a few months for a Peeterman. The Hoegaarden and Leuvens wit were in fact drunk when still fermenting.

Use of "Wind Malt"

The brewers were maltsters at the time. They were making a special malt suitable for the white beers, called "wind malt." It was winter barley (*escourgeon* in French) germinated at cold temperature then dried by the action of wind only (at a temperature as low as seventy-seven to eighty-six degrees Fahrenheit), without any kilning. It was mandatory for the style, and utmost care was taken to produce the palest possible malt. It was then described as being white-ish.

Use of Unmalted Wheat and Other Raw Grains

In all of the white beers, raw grains were part of the grist. It was mainly wheat, but also oat and sometimes—but rarely—buckwheat. The latter would have replaced oats, but it seems that its use was abandoned by most of the Louvain brewers by the end of the nineteenth century. The reason is certainly to be found in the fact that most of those brewers were farmers as well. It was then logical, easier and cheaper to use what they produced locally and without going through a malting process. The malted barley brought the necessary enzymes for the conversion of the starch of the other grains. Those grains brought mellowness, which was sought after for a style of beer in which some tartness or even sourness was present, in order to balance it.

Appendix I

Partial Copper-Mashing with Turbid Mash

As usual in the past, the mashing methods were extremely complex. The mashing-in was made with cold water.

A general mashing method was partial copper-mashing with turbid mash, which means that a part of the wort was pumped, almost unfiltered, in the copper and boiled before returning in the mash-tun. It gave worts with a lot of complex carbohydrates, including dextrins and soluble starch, as the saccharification was incomplete. The dextrins helped the beer to have enough body; the starch played a role in the hazy aspect of the beers.

The spent grains were sparged with boiling water. After that, a part of the boiled wort was filtered, again passing on them, in a "clarification vessel," acting as hop and trub separator. This obviously allowed a lot of tannins from the husks to solubilize, giving astringency (and probably sometimes harshness) to the beer—hence enhancing its refreshing properties.

Short Boiling Time

The boiling was shortened, compared to other beers of the time, which was often immensely long. Often, only a part of the wort was boiled.

The Use of Spices

The Belgian wheat beers are generally associated with two spices: coriander seeds and orange peels (Curaçao). Surprisingly enough, very little mention of spices is made in the old brewing treatises. It doesn't mean that none were used, though. It could have been one of those "brewer's secrets" (a speciality in Belgium), and it seems that coriander, especially, was very often used—but maybe not always. The important thing is that all the records talking about spicing mention very little amounts to be added. The goal was clearly to enhance the flavor, not to overwhelm it.

APPENDIX I

Top Fermentation + Lactic Co-Fermentation, or Spontaneous Fermentation

For the Leuven wit, only top fermented yeast was used (in fact, a leaven), at a low pitching rate, completed by a rapid lactic acid wild fermentation. For the Hoegaarden, the fermentation was totally spontaneous.

The development of lactic bacteria was easy and obviously present in all of the Belgian whites. It was actually the most important benchmark of those beers. The "yeast leaven" used was indeed always heavily infected with *Lactobacillus* and sometimes *Pediococcus*. They were also harbored in the wooden vessels and barrels of the brewery.

On top of that, the bacteriostatic properties of hops couldn't properly act, because:

> *Most of the time, only a third of the worts were boiled with hops.*
> *Only a small amount of hops was added (+/- 160gr/Hl onm average).*
> *The use of old hops was very common.*

The lactic acid was then appreciated for "calming the intestine burning." As the beer was drunk very young, before turning too sour, other microorganisms, like wild yeasts of the *Brettanomyces* species, obviously didn't have the time to develop.

The typical witbier yeast is a "POF+" type of yeast. It means that it produces phenolic compounds during fermentation. It is not surprising, because those yeasts were most probably indigenous wild yeast from the area before being cropped and reused by the brewers. It is well known that the wild *Saccharomyces cerevisiae* are POF+ yeasts.

Haze

The white beers were of course hazy, and their cloudiness was recognized as an important characteristic. It was due to different factors:

> *Colloidal: due to the high protein content of the grains used (wheat, oats, but also winter barley).*
> *Microbiological: from the bacteria, but also from the yeast in suspension. As those beers were normally drunk when still fermenting, the yeast had no time for settling.*

Appendix I

Sometimes provoked, as today: potato starch was sometimes used, only to enhance the haze. Sifted malt flour was also sometimes added in the copper or in the barrel prior to bottling. The tenant would also roll the barrels or gently shake the bottles before serving the beer in order to put back the sediments in suspension.

Low Attenuation, High Carbonation

The attenuation was very low, around 50 percent, allowing the presence of dextrins, which gave mellowness to the beer.

The rest of the extract was high, allowing a secondary fermentation after the cask was bunged up, right before consumption, which gave an abundant head and carbonation.

Density

The density was sometimes as low as 1,018 to 1,020, but the average was closer to 1,035 to 1,040. The density of Peeterman was higher. As the attenuation was very low due to the microorganisms involved and the short shelf life of the beers, the alcohol content was low as well, probably around 2.5 to 3.5 percent ABV on average. Again, the Peeterman was higher.

Vessels & Technology: Rustic!

A lot of vessels were in wood, except for the copper, of course. A coolship was used for cooling. It was often in wood, too. The fermentation took place in wooden barrels, placed upended.

Until World War II, the techniques did not dramatically change.

Refermentation

The white beers were refermented before being sent to the customers. For that, sugar syrup or candy sugar was added before bottling. People liked the beer to be well carbonated, and the "popping" of the bottles at their opening was especially appreciated. If sent in barrels, the refermentation took place inside of them after they were bunged up, thanks to the fact that the fermentation was still active.

THE MAJOR STYLES

A. Bières blanches de Louvain / Leuvense witbieren

Grains: malted barley (45 to 55 percent), unmalted wheat (44 to 56 percent), unmalted oat (6 to 12 percent). Buckwheat was also used, but rarely.

Short boiling time (one hour) for one-third of the wort. The other two-thirds were directly pumped into the coolship, without having been boiled or hopped.

Fermented in four to five days and rapidly sent to the customers to be drunk, ideally eight days after its fermentation. Maximum of conservation: two to three weeks in summer, four to five in winter. Served quite cold.

Characteristics:
Abundant foam
Very pale color
Hazy
ABV between 2.5 and 3.5 percent
Attenuation 50 percent
Lactic sourness (lactic acid: 0.35 to 0.40 percent)
Mellowness
Phenolic off flavors
Refreshing

Until the early 1800s, the malt used underwent a long and cold germination on the floor, then was wind-dried, but it was brewed with its rootlets. This gave a particular flavor, described as herbal, as well as a typical bitterness.

Barley malt and wheat were mashed together.

Lacambre, a brewing scholar and local brewer in the mid-nineteenth century, used the malt without its rootlets and introduced a new technique: the mixed method, in which barley and the wheat were mashed separately.

In the early twentieth century, reports were made of a grist of 40 percent unmalted wheat, 50 percent malted barley and 5 to 10 percent unmalted oat.

Appendix I

The grist was then divided into two parts:

In the mash-tun, a bit of wheat and most of the malted barley. Mashing at cold temperature.
In the boiling kettle, the rest. The rest is cooking.

The mash in the lauter-tun had a high diastatic power and was then sent with the rest into the brewing kettle, to allow saccharification.

As before, only a third of the mash was boiled with hops then sent to the coolship.

B. The Peeterman

The name means "St-Peter's man," as St. Peter (Sint Pieter) was the official saint of the city of Leuven. Peeterman became the nickname of Leuven's inhabitants.

It was darker in color and higher in alcohol (5.0 to 6.5 percent) than the Blanche de Louvain (made in the same region). Its production was similar, but the boiling was prolonged (four to five hours, sometimes even longer). This led of course to more oxidation in the copper and to more Maillard reactions, hence the darker color. The boiling was not only long but also very vigorous, so almost no hop smell could remain. Lime was often added to darken its color, which was more amber. Darker malts were also sometimes used.

The Peeterman had a greater amount of wheat than the Louvain. As for the Blanche, only a third of the wort was boiled with hops. Its density was higher, containing more dextrins, and its taste was a little sweeter, described as almost honey-like.

The hopping rate was higher: 260 to 300gr/Hl for a third of the mash were common. Old hops from the Aalst area were used. As the wort was denser and more hopped, the fermentation took a little bit longer.

When a Peeterman was brewed, the brewer always made a "small beer," called in French the "petite bière Blanche," with the last runnings and the spent hops.

The density of the wort was between SG 1.0587 to 1.0745, or 14.4 to 18 degrees plato. Those are high values for the time in Belgium, but one should take into account the low attenuation yeasts that were used for the white beers. Thus, it doesn't mean those beers were extremely high in alcohol.

Appendix I

The beer was bottled and had to be drunk after three to four weeks during summer and six weeks to two months in the winter, which is a little longer than the Louvain. It remained hazy for a long time.

C. Bière de Hougaerde (or Hoegaerde) / Hoegaardse Bier

For the grist, Lacambre, in 1851, gave the following: five to six parts of "wind" malted barley, shortly germinated, to two of unmalted wheat and one to one and a half of unmalted oat. Malted oat has also been reported to be used. It obviously contained more oats than the Louvain.

Verlinden, in 1933, reported a grist we are more used to, with a balance between malted barley and wheat: 2.5 parts of unmalted wheat to 2.55 of malted barley, 0.5 of malted oat and 0.25 of unmalted oat.

Very rustic brewing methods were used. Wood was present a lot in the utensils and vessels in use: the mash-tun and the coolship were made of it, although some coolships were made of steel. To transfer the wort, buckets were used rather than pumps. For brewing, brewers' paddles were used. In 1909, there were still no engines to be found in any of the fourteen remaining breweries! Each mention in the literature about Hoegaarden says the techniques used for making it haven't really changed, whatever the period we talk about.

The brewing method is, once again, closely related to the one of the Blanche de Louvain.

A third of the wort is boiled with old hops (250gr/Hl) for one hour or a maximum of two hours. All the worts (boiled and unboiled) are then sent to the coolship for cooling and are then transferred in a buffer tank before being put in barrels, without any addition of yeast, to allow a spontaneous fermentation. It makes the historical Hoegaarden the second Belgian beer style to be spontaneously fermented, after the lambic of Brussels. Of course, that spontaneous fermentation exists only for the traditional lambic in Belgium today.

When the fermentation was too slow to start, some brewers immersed baskets on which some "fermentation material," that is, dried yeast and bacteria, was present. The fermentation started almost immediately. Other brewers could add an unboiled portion of wort to boost the start of the fermentation. When they feared a too-strong fermentation (in the summer), they cleaned the barrels more thoroughly. It was as simple as that.

The gravity was around 1.0322 (8.1°P). The alcohol was around 2.5 to 3.0 percent.

Appendix I

The beer, very foamy and sparkling, had clear wheat flavors, acidified quickly and was described as "light, refreshing, agreeable and healthy, with herbaceous flavors," very easy to digest, with a sort of "wildness." In comparison to the white of Leuven and the Peeterman, the Hoegaarden was the sourest, palest and least smooth. As with the Louvain, gelatinized starch was still present in the finished beer. It was served when still fermenting, typically in stone or earthenware jugs, from the barrel, but it was also bottled. It was considered the perfect summer beer.

The beer was sometimes sent to customers after two or three days(!), up to a maximum of fifteen days. It had then to be drunk within eight to ten days in the summer and a bit longer in the winter.

Local customers were said to prefer the beer to be aged a little longer. Its acidity was then more pronounced, and the alcohol content was a little bit higher. The "foreigners" (a term that can mean someone from Brussels as well as from the next village) seemed to prefer the younger, less sour version.

Twentieth Century

During World War I, the production of wheat beer totally stopped, as wheat was kept for making bread. After the war, customers were seeking other sorts of beers (lagers or stronger pure barley bitter ales). Those beers were then drunk locally only.

After the war, a more "modern" method was applied, in some breweries at least, consisting mainly in using metallic kettles instead of wood ones, limiting the time on the coolship and using a second cooling system, more efficient (e.g., the Baudelot type). The recipes were unchanged, but culture yeast was used, even if records show the lactic infection was still present in most if not all breweries. The novelty introduced by Lacambre for those beers (mashing the raw grains in a separate kettle) also became the norm, at least in the bigger breweries with enough money for having more kettles. Nevertheless, the methods remained quite rustic, and it is remarkable to see that, between 1829 (in a book describing methods already in use dating to the late eighteenth century at least) and 1962, when the last descriptions of white beers are made before the renewal of the late 1960s by Pierre Celis, the brewing methods seem to have remained almost unchanged.

Appendix II

A BRIEF HISTORY OF BREWING IN HOEGAARDEN

Not many cities can count over one thousand years of existence. Rome, sure; Athens, of course. But a town of five thousand people in Belgium? That is exactly what the residents of Hoegaarden, Belgium, can claim. Hoegaarden can trace its beginnings back over one thousand years, with the earliest known brewery dating to 1318, according to town records. As discussed in the first chapter, the existence of a stream through town and very fertile farmland provided all the resources the town needed to start its brewing history.

Though the name of that first brewery is unknown, it kickstarted a long, storied tradition in Hoegaarden, the brewing capital of Belgium. Though records of many of these breweries over the last hundred years may not be readily available, some do exist. This appendix will serve as a bit of an overview on brewing in Hoegaarden and focus on twenty-nine of the more recent breweries in town. Recent by European standards, that is.

In 1460, the brothers Beggaarden opened a brewery on Mariadal or Val Virginal. This is where information gets a little scant. After the brothers, the next three hundred or so years saw brewing in the town thrive. The village of Hoegaarden was in the Vrije Heerliikheid (Free Heerliikheid) region, which gave tax breaks to the brewers.

As discussed in the first chapter, Hoegaarden was located in a Liége enclave of Brabant under Austrian rule, allowing the town to trade without restrictions. This made the village a tax refuge for brewers. Around the mid-1500s, Kaiser Karl declared the brewers in Hoegaarden free from all tolls.

Appendix II

Though not from Pierre's brewery, a giant cooper kettle greets Hoegaarden residents and visitors alike as they enter the village. *Courtesy of the author.*

Christine with Juliette in Hoegaarden in 2017. Christine had raised money to bring her father's original equipment back to the United States for her planned Celis brewing museum at the Celis Brewery in Austin. *Courtesy of Christine Celis.*

Appendix II

Pierre being honored by the Order Van Moutstock, one of the oldest brewing organizations in Belgium. *Courtesy Christine Celis.*

In 1560, Kaiser Karl abdicated his throne. Losing a bit of their protection, the brewers in the village organized a brotherhood of brewers. Dubbed the De Edelman Order Van Moutstock, it had the goal of protecting their collective monetary interests. The guild had the duty not only to monitor the quality of the beer, but also to help defend the interests of the brewers.

As an extension of this tradition, the right to brew was passed down from father to son. It was likely one of the reasons why Louis Tomsin, who had no sons of his own, took Pierre Celis under his wing. If you weren't a brewer's son, you married the daughter of a brewer and, by default, could brew yourself.

The village alderman, typically the highest elected official, was always chosen from one of the larger or most prominent brewing families.

From 1740 to 1794, Hoegaarden saw a sort of golden age of brewing. By 1750, out of a population of around two thousand people, there were thirty-nine breweries, with approximately 110 brewers, including malt houses, as most brewers kilned their own malt. If you saw a smokestack attached to a building, chances are it housed a brewery, and many brewers had estate or home breweries that were often in a separate building next to their home.

Appendix II

In fact, there were probably many more breweries than were listed, as many brewers could guest- or contract-brew at other estate breweries.

In 1765, breweries in the village were required to register their equipment, boilers, vats, et cetera. In all, thirty-nine breweries were registered that year, the most in the village's history. They were as follows: Beur Guilliam Janssens, Jacobus Delgré, E.H. Pastor van Overlaar, Nicolaes Van der Molen, Everard Dumont, Widow Bernard Vandermolen, Jean-Baptist Dumont, Jan Babtist Van Ex den Jongen, Servaes Nijs, Jacobus Philippus Cypers, Sieur Hendrick Coenegras, Widow Hendrik Nijs, Widow Marcelis Geerts, Widow Jan Doutremont, Widow Louis Doutremont, Peeter Calu, Bernaert Prinsmel, Bartholomeus Bitches, Jan Baptist Van Ex de Ouden, Jacobus Doutremont, Sieur Servaes Sweerts, Sieur Hendrick Struys, Widow Carolus Van Nerum, Francis Van Autgaerden, Sieur Hubertus Sweerts, Sieur Anthoen Collart Meyer, Anthoen Stockmans, Peeter Taverniers, Jouf die widow Jan Francis Schepers, Francis Labours, Jouf die widow Nijs, Sieur Jacobus Nijs, Gilbert Tossyn, Anthoen Loos, Lamber Dems, Sieur Serves Sweerts, Servaes Van Hagendoren, Christian Groetaers and Sieur Hendrick Struys.

Further flexing their political muscle, brewers in the village built majestic religious squares, as well as a massive and beautifully intimidating brewers' church, Sint Gorgoniuskerk, or Saint Gorgonius Church.

The year 1789 marked the beginning of the French Revolution, leading to events that would soon affect Hoegaarden. By 1794, the village had been annexed, officially ending Austrian rule and spelling the end of coveted monetary privileges the townspeople had enjoyed for so long. The tax breaks had allowed the brewing industry in Hoegaarden to thrive and grow for centuries. Without these favorable tax conditions, brewing began to decline. After the French Revolution, the breweries began to disappear one by one.

At the beginning of World War I, in 1914, there were only eight breweries left (though some evidence suggests fourteen), and after the war, four remained: Cipers, Loriers, Tomsin and Brasseur.

By 1957, only Tomsin's brewery remained, and even he chose to retire. For the first time in over seven hundred years, Hoegaarden was without a brewery, and without its coveted witbier, to boot.

Some of this story you know by now. In 1966, Pierre Celis officially opened his Brouwerij Celis (Celis Brewery), launching the first new brewery in nine years and bringing back the witbier. In 1979, Pierre bought the Hougaardia lemonade factory up the street and moved his brewery. He thrived until 1985, when a fire destroyed the brewery, forcing Pierre to look for money to rebuild.

Appendix II

After effectively being shoved out by the end of that decade, Pierre sold his remaining shares and moved to Austin to open Celis 2.0.

In 2005, the Hoegaarden beer guild began brewing in 't Paenhuys in de Stoopkensstraat (Stoopken Street), and a year later local café (bar) Tavern 't Nieuehuis began brewing.

Let's now take a closer look at a few of the breweries in the village of Hoegaarden's more recent historical record—that is, from the early 1800s to the present day.

Loriers

Standing on the other side of the Nermbeek stream, on Brouwerij Loriersstraat (Loriers Brewery Street), the large Warriors Brewery building towers above the town. The Loriers family began brewing around 1832 and became one of Hoegaarden's most prominent brewing families. They first began contract-brewing at another estate farmer's brewery, until their brewery was finished around 1837. Additions would be done to the brewery, including a tower that was completed in 1930, with the equipment modernized.

As with many things during that time, brewing was done vertically, essentially gravity driven. Loriers reports to have had a boil kettle of 41,250 liters (10,897 gallons). The family made about twenty-two different types of beer, including one known as Hoegaarden Das, which was later brewed in the early 1990s by AB InBev. Not much is known about the style itself, other than that it was an amber-colored beer, and according to Chris Bauweraerts, Mr. Thomas used dried Curaçao peel and coriander when brewing DAS. More than likely, this is also where Pierre decided on Curaçao and coriander for his Oud Hoegaards beer. In fact, Pierre suggested to Bauweraerts that he should add the same Curaçao peel and coriander to his La Chouffe beer at Brasserie d'Achouffe.

Loriers also had a distillery that produced gin and had a water and lemonade division. The Hougaardia factory on Stoopkensstraat, which Pierre Celis would one day move his brewery into, handled anything for Loriers that was not beer.

In 1960, Loriers was acquired by Stella Artois (now AB InBev), which closed it down in 1972. The brewery still stands, but it has since been converted into residential apartments. One of these apartments happens to be occupied by Pierre's wife, and Christine's mother, Juliette Celis.

Appendix II

Gustaff Cipers, Dumont and Vanhagendoren, Ferdinand Van Hogendoren and Oscar Vanhagendoren

Stoopkensstraat (formerly known as Beekstraat) is named after an earthen beer jug that was used to keep beer colder for longer periods. Historically, breweries did not fill bottles but instead focused on kegs, from which beer was emptied into the stoop. Typically, customers would take the stoop filled with beer back home and place it in the ground to keep the beer even fresher.

On the other side of Stoopkensstraat, which one could say was the favored street for the brewers of Hoegaarden, stood Gustav Cipers Brewery, near house number 10. Just down the way from Cipers, at house number 24, was the Dumont brewery. To the left of the Dumont Brewery, between Café Brem (a personal favorite in Belgium to enjoy a beer) and the Kouterhof Tavern, stood the brewery of Louis Vanhagendoren. Cipers, Dumont and Vanhagendoren were at a section of Stoopkensstraat where the stream was made to arch a little, around 1919. As we discussed in part I, water was quite abundant and accessible in this section of town, clearly lending itself to be favored by the brewers. It is near this section of Stoopkensstraat that Pierre's De Kluis Brewery stands (now the AB InBev–owned Hoegaarden Brewery), with a visitor center ('t Wit Gebrouw) that has everything you need to know about the brewing process of their treasured witbier.

The brewery of Ferdinand Van Hogendoren, which stood at house number 53, was the first brewery the Loriers had used, from 1837 to 1885. Van Hogendoren's brewery was later run by a later relative, Jules Vanhagendoren.

At house number 79 stood the brewery of Oscar Vanhagendoren, whose building was demolished in 1993. Not much is known about Oscar, other than that his brewing system produced 2,260 liters per year.

Just past 't Paenhuys stood the brewery of Arnold Cipers, which dated to the mid- to late 1800s. Cipers and his family lived at the nearby farm of Crusbloc (near Tussestraat and Tummestraat). When Cipers passed away, his widow continued the brewing operation, with her son taking over later.

Since Arnold Cipers was a close friend of Louis Tomsin, his widow and Tomsin would often taste each other's beers to ensure that they had the best brew possible. Through it was one of only four breweries in Hoegaarden at the start of World War I, Arnold Cipers's brewery closed in 1940 and was later converted into three brewing garages.

Appendix II

Louis Tomsin

As we cross back over the intersection near Stoopkensstraat and Vroentestraat, on the other side of the white house on the corner, Vroentestraat no. 5 is where the Brouwerij Tomsin was located. As one of the four remaining brewers in Hoegaarden at the start of World War I, Louis Tomsin was already well respected in the Hoegaarden area for his witbier.

Tomsin was the last brewer in Hoegaarden in general, not just of the witbier, and he retired in 1957. With the village having had electricity since 1923, Tomsin built his own electric mill to grind his malt and grains.

Brouwerij Paters Beggaarden

Perhaps Hoegaarden's only monastic brewery, Brouwerij Paters Beggaarden was started by the Fathers of Beggaarden in 1750. The brewery was located across the street from what would be the Tomsin Brewery. The brothers arrived in Hoegaarden ten years earlier. The brewery was operated by the brothers until the end of the French Revolution, when they were expelled from Hoegaarden. After the departure of the brothers, the Sisters of the Sacred Heart took over the brewery, whose beer was later produced at the Brouwerij de Beggaarder.

Brouwerij Van Nerum

Our tour now takes us farther up Vroentestraat and across the street to the right. We now come upon the area where the stream arrives at the Grote Gate. Walking a bit to the right, we arrive at Sint-Cornelishoeve, the large farm brewery of Carols Van Nerum. Van Nerum was a major citizen who commanded much authority in the business of the town.

Appendix II

Brouwerij De Grote Molen

As we make a right on Vroentestraat, we wind around to the De Grote Molen, built around 1249 with the purpose of grinding or milling the malt that the brewers in the village needed. Though the building now serves as apartments, in the 1700s, it served as a brewing complex.

As we walk to the end of the street, we come across the 't Nieuwhuys Brewery, in what locals says is the oldest existing building in Hoegaarden. When it was first built, it was used as a stable for horses and as a coach house.

A fire broke out in the 1600s, and the structure had to be rebuilt. At one point, it was used to entertain traveling military troops, and it housed a cabaret. The basement also contains a Gallo-Roman well. Today, it is used as a café and brewery.

Saint Gorgonius Church

Though not a brewery per se, Sint Gorgoniuskerk (Saint Gorgonius Church) was an integral part of Hoegaarden's brewing history. Located off the main square in the heart of the village, Saint Gorgonius is the brewers' church. Built between the years 1754 and 1759, it is a monument to the brewers themselves and was erected with money from the brewing community.

Built during Hoegaarden's golden age of brewing, it was surrounded by breweries on all sides. The Sweerts family's Ardendnest farmhouse brewery is located next to the chapter house section of the church. With over seven hundred years of brewing heritage, our little trip down memory lane is hardly all-encompassing, but this gives you a little snapshot into a village that literally eats, sleeps and drinks beer.

Appendix III

A BRIEF HISTORY OF BREWING IN AUSTIN, TEXAS

Austin's history is deeply entwined with that of Texas's story of independence. Though these days it is more known for its live music and beer scene, the city was the choice of the fledgling Republic of Texas to be its new capital in 1839, when republic leaders moved it from Houston. Though the central Texas town was first known as Waterloo, its name was later changed to Austin, after the "Father of Texas," Stephen F. Austin, who settled the area in the 1830s with other Anglo colonists.

Over the next few decades, Austin grew in size and importance, though it still lacked one crucial industry that many towns throughout history were founded on: breweries. It wouldn't be until April 14, 1860, that Austin would see its first brewery, founded by German immigrant (I know, shocker, right?) Johann "Jan" Schneider, who came to Texas between 1845 and 1846. Taking out an advertisement in the *State Gazette*, Schneider announced his presence to Texas. Not surprisingly, he brewed the traditional lagers of his native Germany, often touting them as having all-natural ingredients. He likely made the distinction because of a practice in Europe at the time of sometimes mixing narcotics into a beer to increase the intoxication levels.

In 1874, only a few blocks from Schneider's brewery, stood City Brewery, founded by Prussian-born immigrant Frederick W. Sutor, a cabinetmaker by trade. (Prussia would later become part of a unified Germany.) Sutor had arrived in Austin in the 1850s but passed away in 1878, a mere four years after opening his brewery, and it is unknown if his business continued or not. However, by 1885, the former City Brewery building was occupied by a lumber company.

Appendix III

In 1860, another German immigrant, Paul Pressler, began brewing on family land on Manor Road, three miles northeast of the city limits of Austin at that time. He was joined by his brothers Frank and Ernest, and the brothers' brewery, known as Pressler's Beer Garden, was financed by their uncle Charles Pressler, a known mapmaker in Texas.

The Pressler brothers focused on what is now known as steam beer, which features lager yeast fermented at warmer ale yeast temperatures. Today, the term *steam beer* is copyrighted by Anchor Brewing Company in San Francisco, as it was the only brewery to survive Prohibition still making the product. Pressler's Beer Garden would close around 1878, leaving Austin with a brewing gap that would not be filled until the early 1990s. (Yes, Austin's brewing scene is very young, indeed.)

Fast-forward to 1991, and we arrive at a familiar name: Celis. As we know by now, Pierre had moved part-time to Austin and opened his Celis Brewery off Forbes Drive, becoming not only the first craft brewery in Austin but also the first new brewery in the Live Music Capital of World since 1878.

Two years later, Hill Country Brewing and Bottling Company opened off Shady Lane. Opened by brothers Mike and Marshall McHome, Hill Country Brewing focused on classic English-style ales. Though they closed it in 1999, the brothers had become known for their Balcones Fault series of beers, such as Balcones Fault Red Granite and the Balcones Fault Pale Malt. A portion of sales for the Balcones series went to the Hill Country Foundation, an organization whose focus is to preserve plants and animals in the Texas Hill Country.

Though Austin now had two breweries to claim, the brewing landscape would change dramatically in 1993 with the passage of what is known as the "brewpub law," a piece of legislation that made it legal for restaurants to brew and sell their own beer.

The first of these new brewpubs in Austin and Texas in general was Waterloo Brewing Company, founded by Billy Forrester, who had also been the one to introduce the brewpub legislation. Forester owned the now-shuttered Dog & Duck Pub and, later, Billy's on Burnet. Forrester tapped Austinite Steve Anderson as his head brewer for Waterloo.

Waterloo, which opened in December 1993, brewed a variety of beer styles, all named after important places and people in Austin history. There were beers like O'Henry's Porter (a porter named for author William Sydney Porter) and Clara's Clara (a golden ale named for Alamo savior Clara Driscoll). In 2001, Waterloo closed due to rising property values in the area.

Appendix III

In 1994, more brewpubs opened, including the coveted Bitter End Bistro and Brewery on Colorado Street. Like Waterloo Brewing, Bitter End brewed a variety of beers and usually had at least five different varieties on tap, one of which was a Grand Cru, made by head brewer Tim Schwartz, that incorporated many ingredients gifted to Tim by Pierre Celis. Bitter End closed in 2005 after a devastating fire.

Also coming to life in 1994 were brewpubs Copper Tank Brewing Company and Lovejoy's Taproom and Brewery. Located off Trinity Street, Copper Tank was opened by Austin brewing pioneer Davis Tucker and did not add food until two years later. Tucker left in 1996; three years later, he founded North by Northwest Restaurant & Brewery, which closed in the spring of 2020 as a result of the coronavirus pandemic.

Copper Tank's head brewer was Rob Cartwright, who would later go on to open Independence Brewing with his wife, Amy Cartwright. Copper Tank closed its doors in 2005 after filing for bankruptcy.

Lovejoy's opened on Neches Street in downtown Austin. Founded by Chip Tate, Lovejoy's originally started out as a coffee bar that also had a sizable beer selection. Tate, with a push from the owners of a local homebrew shop, converted the kitchen space into a small brewery. Lovejoy's typically carried around thirty beers, again running the gamut of beer styles. In 2012, Lovejoy's closed for good due to rising rent and property values, much as Waterloo Brewing had done.

Already an Austin institution since 1968, the Draught House Pub and Brewery added a brewing component in 1995, adding to Austin's surging beer scene. Still brewing to this day, Draught House, known for a time as Draught Horse, has now been in operation for over fifty years. The quaint European-style tavern is part of Draught House's raw appeal for many. In addition to its many house beers, the pub features a range of beers from breweries around the world.

After the brewpub boom of 1994, a few years passed before any major brewery openings would occur. By the late '90s, two new breweries had arrived on the scene: Live Oak Brewing and Tucker's North by Northwest.

Live Oak, originally located on East Fifth Street, now sits on Crozier Lane in Del Valle, just outside of Austin near the Austin-Bergstrom International Airport. Live Oak Brewing was started in 1997 by homebrewers Chip McElroy and Brian "Swifty" Peters (who has since moved on to the south Austin brewpub ABGB). Live Oak's focus has always been on brewing quality German beers.

Live Oak's attention to detail and unwavering focus on German beers have served it well. In 2015, Live Oak moved to Del Valle, opening a state-of-the-art brewery from the ground up.

Appendix III

Located in North Austin, brewpub North by Northwest was opened in 1999 by Davis Tucker, formerly of Copper Tank. Tucker's new project would seek to elevate the typical brewpub fare by truly marrying the flavors of his beers with that of his food. Despite lasting just over twenty years, North by Northwest closed in April 2020 due to financial challenges that were exacerbated by the economic impact of restaurant closures brought on by the COVID-19 pandemic.

Austin was quiet over the next four years and did not see another brewery open until 2004. From 2004 to 2010, several breweries opened that have now secured their place in Austin's growing beer culture.

By October 2004, Rob and Amy Cartwright had brewed their first batch of beer at Independence Brewing Company. The brewery, which is still located in a warehouse district off Highway 290 in the southeast part of town, started off with the Austin Amber and Bootleger's Brown, two styles no longer common in Austin.

In addition to their brewery, Rob and Amy were a giant force behind the Texas Brewers Festival in the 1990s, as well as the rebooted festival (known as the Texas Craft Brewers Festival) that started in 2011. By 2016, Rob and Amy had sold a minority share of their company to Lagunitas Brewing, a move that bolstered their distribution and allowed for expansion.

Remember Kevin Brand and his (512) witbier that Pierre Celis consulted on? I sure do. (In fact, I think I will go grab one now.) OK, I am back, and we are back to (512) Brewing, founded by Kevin Brand in 2007. (512) gets its name from Austin's area code and focuses on American versions of traditional English and Belgian beers, with a few American styles mixed in. Brand has cautiously grown his brewery over the years, relying on a mainly draft-only model, with bottles mixed in here and there.

From here we will move forward a little faster.

2007

Uncle Billy's Brew and Que was founded by Rick Engel, a Houston native who had opened Houston's first brewpub in 1994. Brian "Swifty" Peters headed up the brewing team, which later included Amos Lowe. With a focus on lager beers, which take more time to mature, like barbecue, Uncle Billy's filled a niche. After all, who doesn't love beer and barbecue? Alas, Uncle Billy's closed in 2019 after a loss in revenue from Celis's bankruptcy. Celis had canned Uncle Billy's mainstay brews for distribution.

Appendix III

2010

Black Star Co-Op opened with a unique business model at the time. Yup, you guessed it, a co-op. Founder Steven Yarak pulled together a group of like-minded folks in 2006 to form their community-owned brewery. Though it is very much a co-op in structure, Yarak and the rest of the co-op board members had to modify the traditional co-op approach to meet the challenges of the beer industry. Black Star still operates today with a variety of styles that appeal not only to beer novices but also to more refined palates.

Brothers Jeff Stuffings and Michael Steffing opened Jester King Brewery with Ron Extract. Jester King's focus from the beginning has been on brewing beers in the Franco-Belgian style, with many traditional styles, like their Black Metal Stout, taking on a new character.

Jester King is a true farmhouse brewery that incorporates local wild yeast into many of its beers and has begun a working farm on the 165-acre property with the goal of using ever-more homegrown ingredients in its beer.

2011

Scott Hovey opened Adelbert's Brewery, a Belgian-style brewery, in honor of his late brother, George Adelbert "Del" Hovey. The focus originated from Del's love of Belgian beers. As you may remember from an earlier chapter, it was Adelbert's Brewery that Christine Celis partnered with to brew the first in her Gypsy line of beers.

2012

Joe Mohrfeld, who cut his teeth as head brewer for Odell Brewing in Colorado, opened Pinthouse Pizza, a brewpub featuring as eclectic a batch of pizzas as beers. Pinthouse now has three locations, with an even larger production brewery in the works, and has won numerous medals. Its Electric Jellyfish Hazy IPA has become one of the most omnipresent local brews in Austin.

Appendix III

2013

Mark Jensen, Amos Lowe and Jill Knobloch opened the Austin Beer Garden Brewing Company (known simply as the ABGB), along with brewing veteran Brian "Swifty" Peters. The ABGB, like Pinthouse Pizza, focuses on pizza as a core component of its menu, though the south Austin brewpub makes lagers, especially pilsners, almost exclusively. ABGB has won numerous awards at GABF and the World Beer Cup.

2015

One of Austin's most centrally located breweries, Zilker Brewing, found its home along a bustling section of East Sixth Street. Brothers Forrest and Patrick Clark and longtime friend Marco Rodriguez founded the urban brewery after getting their start through homebrewing. Zilker stands out because of its sharp branding and focus on sought-after styles such as hazy IPAs and kettle sours.

Blue Owl Brewing made waves when it opened in East Austin in the fall because of its exclusive focus on making sour beers. Customers can expect a surprising range of beer styles that have been made sour with founder and owner Jeff Young's invention of a small stainless-steel contraption, that speeds up the souring process.

2016

When Oskar Blues opened a new location at the end of the summer, Austin became home to one of the country's largest craft breweries. Founder Dale Katechis chose to expand to Texas's capital city because of its laid-back vibe and love of live music, which matches the fun-loving values of the brewery. Oskar Blues is credited with having put one of the very first craft beers into cans—the popular Dale's Pale Ale.

Two veterans of one of Austin's most well-known breweries, Austin Beerworks, split off to open their own venture, St. Elmo Brewing, off South Congress Avenue. St. Elmo makes a range of styles very well, such as the GABF award-winning Roxanne Pink Guava Sour Ale, which visitors can enjoy in the taproom or the large beer garden.

Appendix III

2018

On Hill Country land that was granted to Texas Revolution hero William B. Travis in 1835 stands the scenic Vista Brewing. Founded by Kent and Karen Killough, Vista is not just a brewery; there's also an on-site garden, providing vegetables for the farm-to-table restaurant; an apiary of honeybees; and walking trails that showcase fields of wildflowers in the springtime.

Founded by two brothers, Taylor and Brett Ziebarth, Oddwood Ales has struck a tasty balance between "clean" hoppy ales and funky foeder-fermented brews—sometimes even blending the two. The amibitious beer program is showcased in a family-friendly taproom in east Austin featuring ten different species of wood and a mountain cabin–like feel.

2019

In June, Texas became the final state to allow manufacturing breweries to sell beer to go directly from their taprooms. The law went into effect in September, helping these breweries increase their profit, but it wasn't essential until the coronavirus pandemic shut down on-site dining and drinking in the spring of 2020. Being able to sell beer to go helped many breweries, including Celis, to stay afloat.

2020

The owners behind such popular Austin haunts as the Brew & Brew and Better Half Coffee & Cocktails dived into having a brewery, too. Hold Out Brewing was delayed from opening next door to Better Half by almost two years, and the owners, which include brothers Matt and Grady Wright, didn't let the pandemic get in the way. The Quonset hut and accompanying patio serve up lots of pale ales and burgers, among other pub grub.

Appendix IV

TRIBUTE TO PIERRE

In the early 1990s, my exposure to beer styles beyond the mass-marketed domestic lagers was limited, to say the least. However, after stumbling into the beer business in the summer of '93 by landing a job washing kegs at Otter Creek Brewing in Vermont, that quickly changed. I started to try anything I could get my hands on, and I was fascinated by the diversity of beer styles that were starting to pop up on the shelves.

After washing kegs one day that summer, I stopped by my local store and noticed a beer that I had not yet seen: Celis White. As was the case with all new arrivals, I bought a six-pack. When I got home and poured myself a glass of the cloudy witbier, my first thought was, "What is wrong with this beer?!" I had never seen or tasted anything like it. (Interestingly enough, that was a response I would hear time and time again in the early days of sampling people on Allagash White!) But by the end of the first bottle, I was curious about all of the complex and unique flavors I was experiencing, and I opened a second bottle. Well, that led to a third, and a forth. And by then I was completely in love with the witbier style. In fact, I became so drawn to it that when I started Allagash Brewing in 1995, I made a witbier, Allagash White, our flagship. It was actually the only beer I made at Allagash for quite some time.

For years, I had been eager to meet Pierre and tell him the impact he had had on my life as a brewer. I finally had the opportunity to meet him at the Great American Beer Festival in 2005, when he was introducing

Appendix IV

A celebration for Celis contract beers in Europe around 2005. *Courtesy of Christine Celis.*

his new book, *Pierre Celis: My Life*, a collection of interviews by Raymond Billen. By this time, Allagash had been brewing White Beer for just over ten years, and it was the beer we had become known for. To say I was excited to meet the man who had reintroduced this style of beer to the world—a style that had become such an important part of my life—would be an understatement. And, of course, as anyone who was lucky enough to meet Pierre would tell you, he was more than a pleasure to chat with. He graciously listened to the Allagash story, tried the glass of Allagash White that I had brought over to him and signed a copy of his new book for me.

On a couple of occasions in later years, I was invited to the Celis house in the small town of Hoegaarden, Belgium. (Pierre's daughter, Christine, helped make those visits possible.) It was the very place where Pierre got his start in 1966, and it was fascinating to talk to Pierre and his wife, Juliette, about the early Hoegaarden and Celis years. The highlight of one visit was the opportunity to see the original brewery just across Pierre's courtyard. It was all still there, even the original tiny kettle that had brewed the first batch. Spending a few moments walking around those old dusty brewing tanks, where it all started, was an amazing experience.

Appendix IV

During my last visit to the Celis house, Juliette was kind enough to give me a very old porcelain "Brouwery de Kluis" beer cup, which I now keep next to my desk at Allagash as a reminder of Pierre and the pivotal role he played in brewing history. I'm planning to drink a toast to him with that cup at Allagash's upcoming twenty-fifth anniversary. It was an honor indeed to have known him!

—Rob Tod,
founder, Allagash Brewing, Portland, Maine

Appendix V
COMMON BEER TERMS

ABV (alcohol by volume)—A measure of how much alcohol is in an alcoholic beverage.

Ale—A beer that uses a top-fermenting yeast strain.

Barley—One of the oldest cereal grains in the world, it is the primary source of fermentable sugars in the brewing process.

Barrel—Used to hold and serve beer, but also as a measurement of volume. One barrel equals forty-two gallons.

Blonde Ale—An easy-drinking, light-colored ale with sometimes noticeable spice and fruit notes.

Bock —A dark, multi-German-style ale. The use of the term *bock* in this book does not denote this traditional style.

Boil Kettle—Historically made with many different materials such as copper, these days, boil kettles are mostly stainless steel in origin. Boil kettles boil the wort that will eventually become beer.

Brewhouse— A term that not only refers to the room housing the brewing equipment but also to the growing equipment itself.

Appendix V

Brewpub—Simply put, a brewpub is a restaurant that brews its own beer.

Conditioning—The period in which a beer continues to age, oftentimes adding additional character, as well as the carbonation period.

Draft, or Draught—Typically fresher beer if it is poured from a tap or keg.

Fermentation—The period in which yeast, which has been added after the wort has cooled, begins to eat the fermentable sugars. After consuming these fermentable sugars, yeast converts them into alcohol.

Foeder—A large wood vat, or barrel, that is used to age beer, as well as the site of primary fermentation at times.

Growler—A container often used to fill with beer at the source and taken home.

Hectoliter—European measurement of volume. One hectoliter equals 0.8 barrels.

Hops—The small cones from the hop plant, which, when added to beer, serves to add a bitter character as well as a preservative for the beer. A multitude of varieties exist.

IPA, or India Pale Ale—Though often thought to have been brewed specifically for export to India, IPAs are an ale often quite bitter from the use of large amounts of hops.

Keg—Though kegs come in all shapes and sizes, a keg typically refers to a half barrel, or fifteen and a half gallons.

Lager—A beer that uses a bottom-fermenting yeast.

Malt—Barley that has been "malted," or soaked with water to expose fermentable sugars, often toasted to bring out other characteristics, then used in the brewing process as the main source of fermentable sugars.

Mash—The portion of the brewing process in which the crushed grain is soaked with water to convert the sugars.

Appendix V

Pilsner—A bottom-fermenting style of lager, typically lighter in color and ABV.

Porter—Dating to the 1700s, this is a top-fermenting ale that is lower in ABV and hops than a stout.

Sour—Typically an ale, this is a catchall category for beers that incorporate wild yeast strains and bacteria. Five traditional styles typically fall into this category. These styles have viarying level of tartness and acidity.

Stout—Born from the stronger porters of the mid-1800s, stouts are now distinct in their own right. Typically, stouts can be a little more on the better side coming from the malt used.

Straat—The Flemish word for "street." For example, Stoopkensstraat is "Stoopken Street" in English.

Wheat beer—An ale that is either 100 percent, or a large majority, wheat base.

Yeast—Living organisms that come from the fungi family. These living creatures eat the fermentable sugars pulled from the grain in the mash process and convert them to alcohol.

BIBLIOGRAPHY

Auber, Arianna. "Christine Celis, Uncle Billy's Brew Up New Gypsy Collaboration Beer." *Austin American-Statesman*, September 26, 2016.
———. "Resurrected Celis Brewery Combines Tradition with New Techniques." *Austin American-Statesman*, July 21, 2017.
Austin American-Statesman. "Austin and Texas Beers Rewarded." October 25, 1995.
———. "Brewery May Sit among Hill Country Vineyards." August 6, 1990.
———. "Celis Gets the Gold." October 1992.
Bauweraerts, Chris (founder, Brasserie d'Achouffe), in communication with the author, March 2019–June 2020.
Billen, Raymond. *Pierre Celis: My Life*. Ekeren, Antwert, Belgium. Media Marketing Communications, June 2005.
Bitchbeer.org. *Austin Beer: Capital City History on Tap*. Charleston, SC: The History Press, 2013.
Black, Chris (owner, Falling Rock Tap House), in communication with the author, April 13, 2020.
BOM Brewery. https://bombrewery.com.
Boon, Frank (founder Brouwerij Boon), in communication with the author, June 2019–June 2020
Breyer, R. Michelle "Austin's Beer Makers Are Barreling Along." *Austin American-Statesman*, May 23, 1996.
———. "Celis Sales Roar." *Austin American-Statesman*, June 13, 1997.
———. "A Celis-tial Brew Begins." *Austin American-Statesman*, March 27, 1992.

Bibliography

———. "Celis to Double Production." *Austin American-Statesman*, October 27, 1995.

———. "Something's A-Brewing in Austin." *Austin American-Statesman*, November 2, 1991.

Buchholz, Brad. "He No Longer Brews Full Time, but Celis' Effervescent Passion Remains." *Austin 360*, April 11, 2011.

Camps, Daytona (granddaughter of Pierre Celis; brewer at Celis Brewery), in communication with the author, February 2019–June 2020.

Camps, Gil. *Celis Brewery: A Business History (1992–2000)*. Luven, Belgium: Ku Leuven, 2020.

——— (grandson of Pierre Celis), in communication with the author, June 2019–June 2020.

Camps, Peter (former spouse of Christine Celis, and Celis brewer), in communication with the author, March 11, 2020.

Celis, Christine (chief marketing officer, Celis Brewery; daughter of Pierre Celis), in communication with the author, February 2109–June 2020.

Celis, Juliette (wife of Pierre Celis), in communication with the author, July 7, 2019.

Clarke, Kim (former head brewer and lab manager, Celis Brewing), in communication with the author, April 9, 2020.

Davis, Jason (director of brewing, Freetail Brewing), in communication with the author, May 28, 2020.

Dworin, Diana "Celis Seeking Beer Alliance." *Austin American-Statesman*, November 2, 1994.

Eichenwald, Wes. "Tapped Out: Celis Brewery." *Austin Monthly*, October 2019. https://www.austinmonthly.com.

Farbstein, Brad (founder/president, Real Ale Brewing), in communication with the author, July 1, 2020.

Forrester, Billy (owner, Billy's on Burnett; founder, Waterloo Brewing), in communication with the author, May 25, 2020.

Hieronymus, Stan. *Brewing with Wheat: The "Wit" and "Weizen" of World Wheat Beer Styles*. Boulder, CO: Brewers Publications, 2010.

Historisch Brouwleerpad Hoegaarden. Forest Stewardship Council, 1996.

Houchins, Jim (attorney, founder of Mannekin Brussels), in communication with the author, February 4, 2020.

Hudec, James (director of operations, Celis Brewery), in communication with the author, May 15, 2020.

Janzen, Emma. "Austin's Craft Beer Trailblazer Back Home." *Austin American-Statesman*, July 4, 2012.

Bibliography

Johnson, Pableaux. "Glass of '93." *Austin Chronicle*, April 24, 1998.

Kleck, Wayne (former public relations manager, Celis Brewery), in communication with the author, May 25, 2020.

"Le Bandit Colon." Accessed January 20, 2020. https://sites.google.com/site/atelierdegenealogiedeorpjauche/histoire-de-folx-les-caves/le-bandit-colon.

Leggett, Bob (president, Artisanal Imports; owner, Mort Subite), in communication with the author, February 4, 2020.

Liseron, Mark, "The Resurrection of Celis Austinites Who Shed Many." *Austin American-Statesman*, December 4, 2002.

Mattheson, Miel (former public relations manager, Brouwerij De Kluis), in communication with the author, May 2019–June 2020.

Oliver, Garrett (director of Brewing Brooklyn Brewing), in communication with the author, April 12, 2019.

Reed, Steven R. "Michigan Brewing Company File for Bankruptcy." *Lansing (MI) State Journal*, February 1, 2013.

Tod, Rob (founder, Allagash Brewing), in communication with the author, April 2019–June 2020.

Thompson, Paul. "Celis Brewery Files for Bankruptcy Protection, Heads off Foreclosure Sale." *Austin Business Journal*, July 1, 2019. https://www.bizjournals.com/austin.

Vanderplas, Luc (former jack-of-all-trades, Brouwerij De Kluis), in communication with the author, March 2019–June 2020.

Van Hecke, Bert (owner, BOM Brewery), in communication with the author, May 3, 2020.

Van Mechelen, Luc "BoBo" (former owner, Gambrinus in Austin), in communication with the author, November 9, 2019.

Williams, Diana. "Austin Beers Headed Overseas." *Austin American-Statesman*, September 28, 1993.

———. "Hometown Brew." *Austin American-Statesman*, May 23, 1993.

———. "Roll Out the Celis." *Austin American-Statesman*, February 9, 1993.

Wood, Virginia B. "Daughter of Craft Brewing Pioneer Returns with 'Gypsy Collaborations." *Austin Chronicle*, September 23, 2013.

INDEX

A

ABM. *See* Authentic Beverage management
Adelbert's Brewery 99, 151
Aggie Bock. *See* Celis Brewery
Anderson, Steve 76, 79, 148
Anheuser-Busch 68, 75
Arnauts, Martha 14, 29
at C.R. Goodman 53
ATF 54
Atwater Brewing 101
Austin Beer Garden Brewing Company 152
Authentic Beverage management 93

B

Bauereraerts, Chris 13, 19, 40, 42, 97, 163

Belgium 12, 13, 14, 15, 16, 17, 18, 19, 21, 26, 29, 30, 33, 36, 39, 40, 42, 44, 48, 49, 52, 54, 55, 59, 64, 68, 70, 74, 80, 86, 88, 93, 97, 102, 106, 111, 122, 127, 128, 131, 135, 136, 139, 144
Bière de Hougaerde. *See* Hoegaards beer
Black, Chris 14, 53, 54, 55, 115, 151, 163
Blue Owl Brewing 152
Boelens 64, 65
BOM Brewery 106, 163, 165
Boon, Frank 14, 36, 46, 97
Brabant 15, 19, 21, 49, 127, 128, 129, 139
Brasserie Mont Saint Guibert. *See* Mont Saint Gilbert
brewing museum 60
Brouwerij De Smet 86
Brouwerij Riva 48, 59, 61

INDEX

Brouwerij Van Steenberge 86
Brown Distributing 113
Brusselmans, Vincent 69, 75, 81
Brussels 36, 39, 40, 52, 53, 54, 68, 69, 92, 127, 129, 136, 137, 164
Brusslemans, Vincent 67, 75

C

Café Brem 36, 144
Café 't Nieuwhuys 36
Camps, Daytona 102, 111, 122
Camps, Peter 14, 63, 69, 70, 75, 81, 86, 87, 88
Cartwright, Amy 149, 150
Cartwright, Rob 149, 150
Celis, Ernest 21, 33, 148
Celis, Pierre
   9, 10, 11, 12, 13, 14, 16, 17, 18, 21, 22, 24, 28, 32, 33, 35, 36, 39, 40, 44, 46, 53, 57, 59, 61, 62, 63, 64, 65, 68, 69, 70, 74, 75, 76, 77, 78, 79, 80, 81, 82, 83, 84, 86, 87, 88, 89, 91, 92, 93, 96, 99, 100, 101, 102, 106, 107, 109, 110, 111, 112, 113, 115, 117, 119, 120, 122, 125, 127, 137, 141, 142, 143, 148, 149, 150, 151, 153, 155, 156, 157, 163, 164, 165
Chimay 44, 52, 55, 80
Christine. *See* Celis, Christine
Cipers 142, 144
City Brewery 147
Clarke, Kim 14, 70, 74, 83, 84, 100, 106, 111, 164
Colon, Pierre 50

Coors 55, 68, 77
Copper Tank Brewing Company 79, 149
COVID-19 110, 119, 150

D

D'Achouffe 11, 40, 42, 44, 123
Davis, Jason 14, 79, 83, 89, 149, 150
Daytona. *See* Camps, Daytona
De Baets, Yvan 127
De Kluis 13, 35, 44, 46, 47, 48, 49, 50, 52, 54, 55, 59, 60, 61, 62, 63, 64, 65, 67, 74, 75, 80, 86, 144, 165
Dixie Brewing. *See* Hudec, James
Dog & Duck Pub 148
Draught House Pub and Brewery 149
Duchy of. *See* Brabant
Dumont farm 47, 59, 60
Dumont, Jean-Baptist 47, 142
Duval 55

E

Eastwood, Clint 87
Engel, Rick 100, 101, 150

F

Faux-Le-Caves 94
Flemish Fox. *See* Celis, Pierre
Flemish Fox Brewery & Craftworks. *See* Celis Brewery

INDEX

Forrester, Billy. *See* Waterloo Brewing.

G

GABF. *See* Great American Beer Festival
Gijsegem, Jan van 57, 69, 70, 75
Golden Lager 77, 78, 79
Grand Cru 9, 36, 52, 54, 55, 76, 79, 80, 100, 111, 113, 149
Great American Beer Festival 55, 76, 155
Grottenbier 86, 93, 96
Gypsy 96, 99, 100, 101, 151, 163, 165

H

Hill Country Brewing 79, 119, 148
Hoegaarden 11, 15, 16, 17, 18, 19, 21, 23, 24, 26, 27, 28, 29, 30, 33, 35, 36, 39, 40, 44, 46, 48, 49, 50, 52, 55, 57, 59, 65, 67, 68, 69, 74, 75, 76, 81, 97, 122, 127, 128, 129, 130, 132, 136, 139, 141, 142, 143, 144, 145, 146, 156, 164
Hoegaarden, Belgium 17, 21, 139, 156
Hoegaards beer 16, 27, 129
Hold Out Brewing 153
Houchins, Jim 14, 52, 68, 164
House Bill 1425 79
Hudec, James 14, 119, 120, 122, 165

I

InBev 19, 40, 62, 63, 64, 65, 66, 67, 68, 82, 86, 143, 144
Independence Brewing Co. 150
Interbrew 57, 62, 64, 65

J

Jackson, Michael 54, 82
Jensen, Mark 152
Jester King 151
Johan en de Alverman. *See* Faux Le Caves
Juliette. *See* Celis, Juliette

K

Kanne caves 93, 96
Katholieke Universiteit Leuven 106
Knobloch, Jill 152

L

lambic 40
Leggett, Bob 52, 68, 93, 107, 165
Leinenkugel 81, 83, 89
Lembeek 40, 106
Leuvens Wit 128, 130
Lone Star Brewing 75, 79
Loriers 26, 28, 42, 65, 142, 143, 144
Lovain-La-Nueve University 74
Lovejoys Taproom and Brewery 149
Lowe, Amos 150, 152
Lueven 16, 17, 52

M

Mannaerts, Albert 27
Manneken-Brussels 52
Mason, Bobby 91, 92
Mattheus, Miel 13, 59, 61
Maura 93
Michigan Brewing 89, 91, 92, 100, 102, 165
Midnight In The Garden of Good and Evil. See Eastwood, Clint
Miller 55, 68, 75, 77, 81, 82, 83, 84, 86, 87, 88, 89, 91, 92, 102, 106
Mister Thomas. See Thomas, Marcel
Mohrfeld, Joe 151
Mont Saint Gilbert 28, 42, 44
Moreau, Raymond 28, 42
Mortensen, Brad 100
Mrs. Peters 68
Mulroy, Bill 101
My Life 23, 24, 32, 50, 68, 156, 163

N

New Belgium. *See* Belgium

O

Oddwood Ales 153
O'Henry's Porter. *See* Waterloo Brewing

P

Pale Bock 9, 77, 78, 79, 80, 87, 111, 113
Papazian, Charlie 76
Pearl Brewing 75, 79
Peeterman 16, 128, 130, 133, 135, 137
Peters, Brian "Swifty" 149, 150, 152
Petterman 17
Philip Morris. *See* Miller
Pinthouse Pizza 151, 152
Punksgiving. *See* Celis Brewery

S

Spoetzl Brewing 75
Steffing, Michael 151
Stella Artois 33, 61, 62, 143
St. Elmo Brewing 152
Stoopkensstraat 35, 47, 48, 143, 144, 145, 161
Stuffings, Jeff 151
Surongo 69, 75

T

Tassin, Michael 52, 53, 68, 69
Thomas, Louis 28, 33
Thomas, Marcel 28, 33, 46
Tienen 15, 27, 33, 57, 64, 74
Tod, Rob 97, 123, 157
Tomsin 16, 17, 21, 23, 24, 26, 27, 28, 102, 129, 141, 142, 144, 145
Tomsin Brouwerij 24
Total Beverage Solution 100

INDEX

U

Uncle Billy's Brew & Que 100
University of Texas 52, 68, 70
Usine Meura 30

V

Vader Abt's' Beer 42
Vanderplas, Luc 13, 26, 35, 49, 64, 96, 165
Van Hecke, Bert 14, 106, 110, 111, 165
Vanlangendonck, Juliette 24
Van Mechelen, Bobo 52, 68, 165
Van Moutstock 141
Vista Brewing 153
Vroente 35, 60
Vroentestraat 11, 21, 24, 27, 145, 146
Vuletich, Dally 14, 96

W

Wallonian 51, 86
Waterloo Brewing Company 148
Wayne, Cleck 79
White 9, 11, 40, 48, 74, 75, 76, 77, 78, 79, 80, 84, 86, 88, 100, 106, 107, 111, 113, 122, 127, 128, 137, 155, 156
Wies Anderson Show 76
Winters 46, 62
witbier 9, 16, 17, 19, 24, 26, 27, 28, 29, 33, 35, 36, 39, 40, 47, 54, 55, 61, 64, 75, 76, 77, 89, 125, 132, 142, 145, 155

Y

yeast 27, 28, 32, 42, 44, 59, 70, 78, 86, 100, 110, 111, 132, 136, 137, 148, 151, 159, 160, 161

Z

Zilker Brewing 152
Zolder 30

ABOUT THE AUTHOR

Jeremy Banas is a freelance journalist and beer writer. His writing has appeared in the *San Antonio Current*, *San Antonio Magazine*, TheFullPint.com, *BeerAdvocate Magazine*, *True Brew Magazine*, the *Bexar Times* and the Brewers Association's craftbeer.com, as well as his own website, ruinationpress.com. He is the author of two previous books, *San Antonio Beer: Alamo City History by the Pint* (coauthored with Travis Polling) and *Pearl: A History of San Antonio's Iconic Beer*. He has judged numerous beer competions and hosts beer dinners and lectures. He also serves as a co-founder of San Antonio Beer Week.

Jeremy comes from a proud brewing tradition. His cousins Carl and Joseph Occhiatio were the last owners of the historic Tivoli Brewing Company in Denver, Colorado, from 1965 to 1969, at which his grandfather also worked. Jeremy has achieved the designation of Certified Beer Server in the Cicerone Certification Program and is working toward his master's degree in history. He resides in San Antonio, Texas, with his three boys, Quinn, Jack and Maxwell.

Visit us at
www.historypress.com

www.ingramcontent.com/pod-product-compliance
Lightning Source LLC
Chambersburg PA
CBHW070356100426
42812CB00005B/1524